T0144817

True Tales of Trouble Only
A Best Friend Can Get Away With

Douglas E. Brown and Kaori A. Brown

HOWELL
BOOK
HOUSE

Howell Book House
a division of
IDG Books Worldwide, Inc.
An International Data Group Company
Foster City, CA • Chicago, IL • Indianapolis, IN
• New York, NY

Howell Book House
IDG Books Worldwide, Inc.
An International Data Group Company
1633 Broadway
New York, NY 10019

Howell Book House is a registered trademark under exclusive license to IDG Books Worldwide, Inc., from International Data Group, Inc.

Library of Congress Cataloging-in-Publication data:
Brown, Douglas E., 1962–
   Bad dog!: true tales of trouble only a best friend could get away with / by Douglas E. Brown and Kaori A. Brown.
   p. cm.
ISBN:978-1-62045-764-1
   1. Dogs—Behavior—Fiction. 2. Humorous stories, American. I. Brown, Kaori A. II. Title.
PS3552.R68545 B342000
813'54—dc21   99-048250

For general information on IDG Books Worldwide's books in the U.S., please call our Consumer Customer Service department at 1-800-762-2974. For reseller information, including discounts, bulk sales, customized editions, and premium sales, please call our Reseller Customer Service department at 1-800-434-3422.

Manufactured in the United States of America

Contents

	Acknowledgments	iv
	Dedication	v
	Preface	vii
Chapter 1:	Plumbing	1
Chapter 2:	In the House	9
Chapter 3:	Clothing and Accessories	23
Chapter 4:	Food and Water	29
Chapter 5:	Doggy-Do	49
Chapter 6:	Flatulence	63
Chapter 7:	In the Yard	69
Chapter 8:	Confinement	85
Chapter 9:	Cars	97
Chapter 10:	Off to the Vet	111
Chapter 11:	Owners and Training	121
Chapter 12:	Trouble with the Law	131
Chapter 13:	Jealousy and Embarrassment	139
Chapter 14:	Oops!	159
Chapter 15:	Beyond Categorization	169
	About the Bad Dog Chronicles Gang	181
	Please Share with Us and *Vote for the Baddest Dog in the Book*	184

Acknowledgments

We would like to thank Maggie for destroying our house and making this book possible. A big thank you to Karen Bannan for including Bad Dog Chronicles in the *PC Magazine* Top 100 List of Web sites, Adam Stiles for being the first Internet service provider for www.baddogs.com, Suzanne Leonard for the beautiful dog portraits on the Web site and her support, Brigitte Kersten-Riggs for her help with the Web site, Steve Foley for helping produce the "Bad Dog Chronicles Tails of Woe" video, Anthony Brajevic for the financial support to keep Bad Dog Chronicles on the Internet and all the Bad Dog Chronicle Web site fans.

Thank you to Dominique DeVito for discovering our Web site and approaching us with this book idea and to Amanda Pisani for being a terrific editor! Although it was a lot of hard work and weeks of sleepless nights, it was a pleasure compiling and writing this book.

We'd also like to thank our families and friends, who probably thought we were a little crazy when we first came up with the idea for the Bad Dog Chronicle's idea, for all their support. We finally did it!

The biggest thank you goes out to all the story and photo submitters. We thoroughly enjoyed reading each story and appreciate your support.

Dedication

To Our Son:
Jae-Sun Chan-Young Brown

In Memory of Lucas
and Honey Bear

Preface

Left to right—
Maggie, Emily,
Andrew

We at Bad Dog Chronicles are on a mission for "dogkind." We believe that it is every dog's right (if not every dog's innermost need) to destroy humans' belongings. For far too long we have "obeyed" our humans. We "obey" so much that we even allow them to choose "our" mates.

To stop this madness, we at Bad Dog Chronicles have created this "How-To/Self Help" book to get you on your way to happy badness. In this book, you will find stories from all kinds of bad dogs—big dogs, small dogs, young dogs and old dogs. They are dogs from all over the world, representing many breeds and doing all kinds of bad deeds.

These stories are written straight from the "dog's paw" and will describe how each dog did its bad deed, how it felt and the resulting reaction of its owner. Most importantly, the stories will give you the "dog's perspective" on why these events happened.

Once you read this book, you, too, will be inspired to destroy your home, yard or car. You will feel terrific once you start to apply some of the techniques you find in these pages.

We dogs have remained silent for far too long. In this book, we are providing a forum for dogs to finally speak out. We at Bad Dog Chronicles hope you feel empowered after reading this book.

Ruff,
Andrew, Emily and Maggie Brown

CHAPTER 1

Plumbing

Don't Leave the Bathroom Door Open!!!

Kody and Chris

Dog's Name: **Kody**
Breed: **Labrador Retriever**
Age: **3 years**
Sex: **Male**
Owner: **Chris Stagg**
Location: **Sparwood, B.C., Canada**
Damage: **$32,000**

My dad used to take me to work with him every day. One day, however, the forestry company my dad works for decided to implement a "No Dog" policy. From that day on, I had to stay at home. I wasn't too happy about this change, but I'm a good guy and decided to just put up with it.

About a month went by and staying at home was getting very boring. My dad was usually gone for 5 to 10½ hours. On the day in question, my boredom got the better of me and I decided to check out the house.

I went into the main bathroom to see if I could find Kleenex to tear up and the door closed behind me!!! Well, I panicked! I tried to get out in every way imaginable. I tried the door, the walls, the counter, the toilet . . . Uh-oh . . . the toilet broke. Water was spraying everywhere! I was getting soaked.

I figured the door just had to be the way out so I gnawed on the doorknob until it gave. Freedom! I hoped my Dad would come home soon. His house was filling with water pretty fast.

It was 4:30 and it had been about eight hours since the toilet broke. Everything was very wet. The house began to creak and moan. 5:30 . . . No Dad yet. He was unusually late. 6:30 . . . Dad at last!!! He would make everything better. He seemed pretty mad—psychotic even!

He couldn't find any help because it was the Friday of the August long weekend. I decided I'd better just stay out of the way!

In the end I had become a very expensive dog. The basement settled four inches with the weight of the water and the upstairs floor settled in turn.

After repouring the basement, refinishing the interior, re-doing the bathrooms, etc., the grand total came to around $32,000.

The moral of the story? Don't leave the bathroom door open when you leave your best buddy at home during the day!

Misha

Dog's Name: **Misha**
Breed: **Siberian Husky**
Age: **1 year**
Sex: **Male**
Owner: **Cynthia Tumiel**
Location: **Texas**
Damage: **$250**

My human mom's garden hoses have always been great fun. They are fun to chew on—especially when my human is trying to sprinkle the lawn and I can get water to squirt out through the holes I make. I also like it when my human sprays me with the hose.

One night, when I was about a year old, I figured out how to turn on the water myself! I tugged and I tugged on the hose and finally the faucet and pipe snapped off the back of the house.

Boy, did water spray out then! It was great! My mom wasn't too happy, though. She came out into the yard in her pajamas and nearly had a heart attack.

She made a couple of telephone calls to plumbers and I heard her yelling at them about why they advertise that they have 24-hour service when they really don't have anybody around at 3 a.m.

She went out to the curb to try to turn off the meter herself and couldn't do it. Finally, she had to call one of her male coworkers and wake him up so he could drive over to turn off the water.

This guy doesn't have dogs and he doesn't understand what my mom sees in me. I had to buy him a nice bottle of wine out of my doggie treat fund to apologize for getting him out of bed.

The next day a plumber finally did show up, and boy, was he impressed. He owned Dalmatians, a breed that is unfairly credited with being the most ingenious and destructive. But he had to admit that even his dogs had never done what I did. They only tore the siding off the house and real predictable stuff like that.

Oh, yeah, now Mom unscrews the hose from the faucet when she's finished using it. And she keeps it coiled in a big heavy clay thing that's hard for me to get into. But I'm bored with hoses. Now, I'm into upholstery!

Diamond

Dog's Name: **Diamond**
Breed: **English Springer Spaniel**
Age: **Puppy**
Sex: **Female**
Owner: **Nick Campinelli**
Location: **Los Angeles, California**
Damage: **$5,000**

My name is Diamond and my sister's name is Star. Our owner wanted to go away for a few days so he called a friend of his and asked him whether he would take us for just two days.

Being a good Spaniel person, of course he said yes. We were just having a ball running around on the beach as he lived near the ocean. We were dead tired that evening and the friend wanted to go out to dinner but didn't know what to do with us. We seemed pooped so he put us in the guest bathroom and left.

Now, we are puppies, you know, and can recover rather well, so we started to investigate this small room and found these little white things under the sink.

I bit into one and it was soft, so I chewed some more. It wasn't long before water started to drip and the drip got bigger and bigger until it was a spray. We started to get really wet so we hid behind the toilet. I thought that there was a lot of water in the ocean but, man, this was a flood!

Maybe an hour went by before we heard some terrible noise. The guy and his wife got home with the water flowing out the front door, the back door, the porch door and onto the rug. Boy, were they mad at us over just a little white hose.

Dog's Name: **Albert**
Breed: **Labrador Retriever**
Age: **4 years**
Sex: **Male**
Owner: **Russell**
Location: **Wellington, New Zealand**
Damage: **$5,000**

Most days I like to chew branches on my owner's trees, which he kindly puts in my backyard. That is until he pruned them all, and I couldn't reach the branches any more.

However, being an imaginative wee soul, I hunted for a replacement chew, and found it in the toilet overflow pipe.

It crackled and crunched quite satisfactorily. Then, it came right out of the wall. Never mind. Good while it lasted.

Weeks passed . . . months even. Then one day, while passing the back of my owner's kennel, I heard a thud, and noticed my owner's leg poking right thorough the floor. In fact, my owner was still sitting on the toilet, which had also gone through the floor.

Seems that over the months, the steady drip-drip of the overflow pipe had gone into the wall and soaked through the chip-board floor, under the vinyl. It spread through the floor in the adjacent rooms and eventually it all crumbled away like a soggy Weet-Bix.

Being gradual water damage, it wasn't covered by insurance either.

Note for those overseas dogs: Weet-Bix is a local breakfast cereal a bit like a large biscuit, made of compressed wheat flakes. Chip-board is a compressed fiber-board flooring commonly used in New Zealand.

CHAPTER 2
In the House

Joe

Joe's handiwork

Dog's Name: **Joe**
Breed: **German Shorthaired Pointer**
Age: **4 years**
Sex: **Male**
Owner: **Paul Labas**
Location: **New York**
Damage: **$10,000**

My owner had gotten up early to head off to work, and, as always, he put the trash container on the counter, knowing I couldn't reach it as I was only a pup then.

As he left the house, I noticed that the can was located close to the edge of the counter. With one swift leap I jumped for it. The container tipped over onto Paul's kitchen stove and I received some real tasty breakfast leftovers.

While I was dining, I hardly noticed that when the can landed on the stove it hit one of the buttons and somehow my feast began to smoke. The smell of burnt plastic quickly turned into a fireball that eventually engulfed the entire kitchen.

Luckily Paul's neighbors saw the smoke and rushed right over and let me outside. The fire trucks were a real sight to see, so pretty red and flashy. The firemen put out the fire and a special fire investigator arrived at the same time Paul did.

They went into the house and I followed. Paul was hugging me and telling me how glad he was to see that I got out alive. As Paul and the investigator searched for the cause of the blaze, their eyes slowly focused on what looked like a melted trash container all over the stove.

As Paul talked to the investigator he just shook his head and laughed and said that *I* caused it!!! The investigator stared at Paul with disbelief and searched around until he finally agreed with him.

The insurance people must not like me as they told Paul that they would not insure him anymore unless he got rid of me.

I'm glad to say that now I am allowed to roam anywhere I want when Paul's not at home because instead of locking me in he locks me outside, except when it rains. Then he opens the garage for me to stay dry.

Paul seems to enjoy his new kitchen and now has a stove that turns itself off when not in use!!!

Jake and Woody

Dog's Name: **Jake**
Breed: **Golden Retriever**
Age: **Puppy**
Sex: **Male**
Owner: **Georgia Lynch**
Location: **Latham, New York**
Damage: **$1,000**

Mom and Dad left my "twin" brother Woody and me with John, the "baby-sitter," and went to North Carolina to visit their sons.

We had our very own room to play in with lots of chew toys and comfy blankets for our naps. John the baby-sitter would come to feed us and let us out to play in the backyard. Well, several days passed and we started getting pretty bored. We discovered that we could squeeze into a lot of different spots in our room.

Behind the washing machine there were tons of nice cold pipes we could lick. Sometimes we would slip and "accidentally" get a chuck of wallboard. We found that if we chewed the wallboard enough we could actually see into the next room. We kept chewing and scratching and made the hole big enough to crawl through. The bathroom!!

The bathroom door was open and we made our escape into the rest of the house. We had a ball—we ran *all over* the place. We ate carpeting, one whole door and part of the stairway. Later that day, John came back to let us out. *Boy*, was he surprised. You should have heard all the very loud words he said—nothing like we'd ever heard before. You should have heard him when he discovered our new "doorway" to the bathroom.

John fixed it so our access to the bathroom was cut off, and my twin Woody thought we had no way out. I figured if we did it once, we could do it again—I'm no quitter! This time I tried a different approach—next to the furnace—wood paneling!! Now that's a pretty good item to chew, but you gotta watch those splinters.

Well, you would have thought Woody and I became full-fledged beavers that day. You could have built a dam out of the wood we gnawed. Needless to say, John repeated the same words that day, too. He spent the next several hours barricading the walls with anything he thought was unchewable. We knew his nerves were going fast now.

When Mom and Dad came home and saw all the holes in the walls, they had a *fit*—especially Dad. Mom had to re-wallpaper the entire bathroom because we ate the wallpaper and border along with the wallboard on our first break out.

For the time being I'm just waiting for them to go away again—and hope we have the same sitter—John.

Tsar, left; Cleo, right

Dog's Name: **Cleo**
Breed: **English Springer Spaniel**
Age: **Puppy**
Sex: **Female**
Owners: **Victoria Tong and Chuck Bennett**
Location: **Ohio**
Damage: **$10**

Cleo here. I'd like to tell you about the time my brother and I decided we wanted to go hunting. Being Springer Spaniels, we are bird dogs, but our dad had been doing some other hunting for something called a deer and we were *not* invited! Imagine!

Tsar and I were still puppies then, but we had graduated from being kept in the kitchen with a dog gate (way too easy to climb) to being locked in the bedroom while Mom and Dad were out.

Well, one morning, Mom and Dad left for work, as usual, and we were amusing ourselves with the pillows on the bed. I got bored and decided to check out the closet. Mom and Dad no longer left out any yummy shoes or such, but we did find the big box.

With some difficulty, we managed to drag the big box out of the closet and get the top flaps open. Inside was the most amazing assortment of stuff all covered with what looked like leaves and which smelled really delicious! Hats, gloves, a jacket and inside one pocket were some squishy tubes with screw-on caps.

Caps (ha ha)—no problem, just bite! I bit brown and black, Tsar got green and tan. We had a great time painting extra spots on us! We started looking like Dad's hunting clothes. Maybe now that we could hide in the forest he would take us with him. But wait! We still smelled like dogs. Where is it, where is it, that bottle of great smelling stuff? *There—in the bottom of the box!*

Our salvation! Just a little behind each ear! Wait your turn, Tsar! You're gonna spill it!!!!! Oh great, Tsar, you got it all over the bed. Here, use the pillows to soak it up. Maybe they won't notice, but my, doesn't it smell really heady in here?

When Mom and Dad got home there was H*** to pay, though they liked the camouflage jobs. We all slept in the living room for a week while the bedroom aired out. The neighbors thought Mom and Dad were crazy to have the bedroom windows open in mid-December.

I don't know about you, but Tsar and I still get all excited when we smell that stuff. Just what is "Doe-in-Heat" made of, anyway?

Gracie with friend

Dog's Name: **Gracie**
Breed: **Italian Greyhound**
Age: **1 year**
Sex: **Female**
Owners: **Kristen and Alexandra Hichcock**
Location: **Conway, Arkansas**
Damage: **$500**

Hi, my name is Gracie. I'm a totally spastic little dog (only 7 pounds), but I am incredibly resourceful for my size. By the way, big dogs, I bet you couldn't pull off my trick, so size isn't everything!

My mom, my sister and I live in an 82-year-old house that Mom has been renovating for years. A little background: This house sat vacant for four years before Mom bought it. I guess those dumb-looking squirrels in the yard are actually smarter than they look, because they were smart enough to realize that big old house was going to waste sitting vacant all those years, so they abandoned all the trees in the yard and moved in!

This past summer, Mom hired a couple men to help with the last two big jobs—renovating a bathroom and the kitchen. One day, she came home at lunchtime to check in on the guys and to let me out of the kitchen (my personal prison) for a while.

We ran upstairs to see what the guys were doing in the bathroom. They were in the process of tearing out the old walls . . . *Eureka!* Squirrel graveyard! I found it first, so as far as I was concerned, it was mine! I grabbed a squirrel carcass and ran downstairs with it.

While Mom was chasing me around yelling, "Gross! Gracie, drop it! Da**it! Drop it, Gracie!" the guys upstairs cleaned out the other three carcasses. Mom caught me, and discarded my mummified squirrel.

The guys (ha ha ha ha . . . fools) put the other three in the debris pile they were creating from their demolition. While Mom and the guys were talking about the work, I was busy removing the squirrels from the debris pile and putting them back in their little graveyard. I had always heard it was bad to disturb the dead! It was so easy to do! I just walked back and forth in between their feet and they never even noticed me!

Well, sometimes my memory is a little like a human's—I forget things, but eventually they come back to me. One day I remembered my stash. Mom and my sister were busy downstairs so I went upstairs to check things out.

It was a very long time before anyone came upstairs. It was my sister, Alex. The little rat fink . . . all the way back downstairs she was screaming, "Uh oh, Mommy, Gracie made a mess!" Well, what do you expect?! How can these people expect me to check in on the graveyard and pay my proper respects when they've put up Sheetrock, plastered, painted and hung wallpaper!

Oh well, maybe it will be easier to visit next time . . . wherever they are. I noticed Mom took them outside somewhere before she called the guys to come back and repair the walls.

Left to right: Conan, Dylan, Harley

Dogs' Names: **Dylan and Harley**
Breed: **Mixes**
Ages: **1 year**
Sexes: **Male and Female**
Owner: **Barbara McMurray**
Location: **Arizona**
Damage: **$100**

My name is Dylan and I have a littermate, Harley, and our sister from our mom's second litter is Conan the Destroyer. Our adopted parents, Barb and Joe, fail to recognize our talents as contractors.

Before Conan arrived, Harley and I decided to remodel the doghouse Joe built us. There were a few things that just weren't right. And we needed something to do after digging up the yard, anyway.

I removed the carpeting, strand by strand. I had at least a hundred feet of carpet yarn dragged all over the yard. Then, I started widening the doorway (I have put on a few pounds since Barb had me neutered—I got her back for that). I also chewed the lattice panels off of the porch. (Bitter Apple tastes great!)

Harley needed a deck to sunbathe, so she removed the shingles from the roof. Those shingles are a bit warm in our desert climate and they make great chewy toys. Harley also uses the new deck to keep an eye on the neighbor's barbecue.

When Conan arrived, she dug out the basement and assisted with the doorway. Conan prefers gardening, but does contracting in her spare time.

We decided we wanted air-conditioning in our house and sent Conan to disconnect Barb and Joe's AC unit.

She had chewed through the wires, and when we went back to get it, there was a fence around it. Joe built us a bigger house, with a wide doorway and no carpeting.

We are thinking of improvements we can make to our new home. We have a few great ideas for Barb and Joe's house, if only they would leave us alone inside for a while.

Gus, member of Gang of Four

Dog's Name: **Tia**
Breed: **English Cocker Spaniel**
Age: **5 years**
Sex: **Female**
Owner: **Anne Pilaro**
Location: **Maryland**
Damage: **$250**

I am Tia, Queen of all I survey. I rule the roost here at home along with my four boys and my non-fuzzy mommy. I have to tell you what my sons have done, because human Mommy is *so* mad, she can't even talk right now!

My human mommy was having a bad day. She went outside to get the paper and locked herself out of the house when the twins (Teddy and Gus, 8 months old) closed the door behind her. Oops!

When she went out, she hadn't kenneled up any of the boys! While Mommy went to find help to get back inside, the twins got up on the couch and dug a hole in the arm, completely shredding the fabric and the foam and springs underneath.

In the meantime, my two older boys (Taz and TeeJay, 2 years old) got into the kitchen and knocked over the food bin. TeeJay, who is a stomach on feet (he gets that from his father, *never* from *me!*) ate almost four pounds of kibble. Taz had a great time "hoovering up" after him.

After the babies destroyed the couch, they started on Mommy's briefcase and shredded a whole file she had brought home to work on. Then Gus knocked the baby gate down and went upstairs, where he bit into my pillow and pulled all the stuffing out.

Of course, I had *nothing* to do with all of this; I stayed on my throne and watched the whole thing.

When Mommy finally came in, she put the "gang of four" in their kennels for the rest of the afternoon, while I showed her what a mess they had made! I know Mommy loves us all, but there are times when I think she should have sold off all of these brats.

If I had my way, I would *love* to be an only dog again!

The Dog Burglar

Nicki

Dog's Name: **Nicki**
Breed: **Bouviers des Flandres**
Age: **6 years**
Sex: **Female**
Owner: **Julie Silva**
Location: **California**
Damage: **$250**

My mom used to work swing shift for ambulance dispatch. Even though I was on guard duty outside, Mom would call and listen from her answering machine, monitoring the room. One night Mom called and could hear someone stomping around the house, slamming doors and just making all sorts of noise. Mom put a fellow dispatcher on the room monitor and called the police.

Mom, all you had to do was ask why I needed to rip the screen and jump in through the window. The police officer laughed and just left me inside until Mom got home. While I was in there alone I got sort of nervous, knocking things over and eating Mom's brand-new glasses. The things on the table were just an accident, they just got thrown away so they must not have been important.

The screen was no big deal to fix—Mom had a lot of experience before this. Sorry, Mom. And now I have a rap sheet . . .

CHAPTER 3
Clothing and Accessories

Pearl Poots

Dog's Name: **Gracie**
Breed: **Dachshund**
Age: **Puppy**
Sex: **Female**
Owner: **Julie W. Smith**
Location: **Hoopeston, Illinois**
Damage: **$250**

One day, when I was but a puppy, I was doing my customary investigating of all the tabletops in the house. I used to jump up on chairs and climb up from there to the tabletop.

Well, on one rather large table, I found a cloth bag. It was small and smelled interesting, so I chewed it until it opened. Then, this long string of white beads came out. I had never seen anything like it before!

It smelled really interesting, too, not like food exactly, but definitely like something I wanted to chew on! So I did. Of course, I have to say that *everything* smells to me like something I want to chew on!

To my surprise, the string fell apart in short order, and I wound up swallowing many of the funny beads, although I did not swallow the string or this metal clasp thing that was attached to the string.

Then my human daddy, who had been napping, came into the room, and there I was, surrounded by . . . evidence! He let out a yell. *"You hound from @#%$! Those were my mother's pearls!!"*

I found out that these things were called pearls, that they grow inside of these funny creatures called oysters and that humans have an attachment to things that belong to dead folks. A learning experience for sure. I also "pooted" pearls. I may have had the most valuable "poot" in the world!

I Eat Teeth!

Dog's Name: **Thibault**
Breed: **Blue Heeler**
Age: **1 year**
Sex: **Male**
Owner: **Steven S. Carter**
Home: **Burnaby, B.C., Canada**
Damage: **$500**

I found the coolest chew toy lying on "my" side of the bed. It had this row of white things attached to a pink base. My owner had been out that night having fun without me, so I think he brought it home as a special treat for me. How thoughtful!

Not too tasty, but it was kind of crunchy and also chewy. An experience that is hard to define, but I enjoyed chewing it to tiny bits!

In the morning, my owner woke up and walked into his bathroom looking for something.

Well, hmm, he said . . . They aren't in the glass where I usually leave them soaking. Where the heck did I leave them? In the living room next to the half-devoured pizza? No. In the kitchen? No, not there. Could they maybe be on the nightstand by my bed? Nope . . .

Oh no, he said. Maybe he wore them to bed and they fell out. He looked under his pillow and found the upper one. But where is the lower . . . ?

Gulp! Uh oh! That couldn't have been . . . I thought as I acted like I was still sleeping.

There it was in tiny little pieces! He found *it* and I had eaten almost all of it! All that remained were a few bits of pink and white tooth bits littered throughout "my" side of the bed.

It cost my owner $500 Canadian to replace it, but he never even said "Bad Dog!" to me 'cuz he knew it wasn't my fault.

How was I supposed to know that humans' teeth fall out of their mouths like that?

Guiness

Dog's Name: **Guiness**
Breed: **American Staffordshire Terrier**
Age: **Puppy**
Sex: **Male**
Owner: **Brigette Kersten-Riggs**
Location: **Oklahoma**
Damage: **A Dozen Missed Phone Calls**

Hi, I found this strange thing that buzzes and vibrates. Sometimes it beeps. Mom calls it Dad's pager for work.

Well, I was hanging out on the Lazy-Boy taking a nap when I heard this noise. It stopped; then, after a few minutes, I heard it again. After a while, the thing making the noise fell off the TV, so I went to investigate it.

I bit it while it was buzzing and it finally stopped. After about five minutes, it started again, so I bit it again. This went on for about two hours.

Well, when Mom came home at lunch time to check on us, she found it in my mouth. Oops—I was in trouble. I put lots of teeth marks on it and she called Daddy. Then she turned it off.

I wonder if he will leave it around again. Hmmm . . . I also destroyed one of Dad's model BMW cars that he keeps on this shelf with lots of other little toys. They might be fun some day!

I hear talk of a gate that's going to be installed at the top of the stairs to keep me off the bed; this could be a new challenge. And can anyone tell me why Mom now hides the trash in the closet?

Well, it's time to attack another one of Dad's little cars . . .

I Hear You Loud and Clear

Dog's Name: **Jenna**
Breed: **Portuguese Water Dog**
Age: **6 years**
Sex: **Female**
Owner: **Christi Overton**
Location: **Oak Harbor, Washington**
Damage: **$1,000**

My name is Jenna. I have been told that my breed is a "mouthy" one. In our homeland, we are known to carry floats and nets, swim from boat to boat and herd fish. Not having that opportunity here, I have had to resort to creativity that includes just about anything I can get my mouth around.

In my house, wastebaskets are just decorations. My mother now owns stock in those companies that make chew items. My shopping list has become quite long, but let it suffice that I always run and hide when my human is out cleaning up the yard, because I always have surprises for her!

I performed my greatest feat one day when my human great-grandpa was visiting. I figured anything in a dish located on a table was fair game. I didn't see what the big deal was until Mom got a call at work from Grandpa and I heard him say, loud and clear, "I think the dog ate my hearing aids."

I knew I was in trouble when she came home and began tearing the house apart, and then came the frantic phone call to the vet. He, of course, was laughing really hard. Mom was not.

Yard patrol was not too much fun that week, especially when she found the two crunched hearing aids a few days later. This particular episode replaced her fury over the diamond earrings.

CHAPTER 4
Food and Water

Kid

Dog's Name: **Kid**
Breed: **Kuvasz**
Age: **4 years**
Sex: **Male**
Owner: **Michele Valesano**
Location: **Lower Lake, California**
Damage: **Nothing That a Few Months of Therapy Couldn't Cure**

had only been in my new home for about six months. I really loved my new family, especially my little girl. She's 5 years old. She always gives me a lot of treats.

One day, my man came out to my yard and dug a hole. I couldn't understand this because he gets mad when I do it. His hole wasn't very big, and mine usually are, so I guess that's why it's okay for him to dig.

Anyway, after he finished his hole, he went back into the house. I could hear my little girl crying; it really upset me that she was sad and I couldn't go to comfort her.

After a little while, my man, woman and little girl came out of the house. My little girl looked so sad, but she wasn't crying anymore. I tried to think of some way to make her happy again. Then I saw that she was holding something out in front of her. Her hands were open, so I knew it must be a treat. She's always so happy when I take a treat from her hands.

I ran up to her and acted like I was all excited, because she always laughs when I act goofy. I guess because I'm so tall. I'm 30 inches at my shoulders and weigh 125 pounds—about two or three times as much as she does.

Anyway, I grab my snack from her hands and she starts crying again. Then she starts yelling. My man must have wanted to make her laugh, too, because he starts chasing me all over the yard.

We play like this a lot and my little girl *always* laughs, but not this time. "Look, little girl," I call to her, "I'm eating my treat. See? Just like you want me to. Why aren't you happy, now?"

Meanwhile, I'm thinking that she should have taken the feathers off before she gave it to me. It was a pretty good snack, but it did remind me of my little friend who used to sit in the window and sing to me.

I can't wait to see him today. Maybe he knows why our little girl was so sad? *Burp* . . .

Bridget

Dog's Name: **Bridget**
Breed: **Labrador Retriever**
Age: **4 months**
Sex: **Female**
Owner: **Margaret Norton**
Location: **Urbana, Illinois**
Damage: **Altered Scientific Data**

My mother adopted me when I was a tiny puppy and she was a graduate student studying how fruit grows. It's a good thing for her that I was born with an appreciation for fine food, such as pizza, dead mice and fruit. Especially fruit, because that meant I could really help her with her field research.

When I was 4 months old, she took me out with her to pick strawberries for something called a "yield trial." That's where you pick all the berries and weigh them to see how much the plants produce.

She got down on her hands and knees to pull the berries off the plants and put them into little boxes to be weighed. I thought that was too much work. It was much easier to take the berries out of the other people's boxes. They didn't mind at all. In fact, it made them so happy that they jumped up and down and shouted. It wasn't my fault that they forgot to weigh me before I ate all those strawberries.

I also helped during blueberry season. (But they forgot to weigh me, again.) I ate a *lot* of blueberries. Later that day, when my mom took me outside, I pooped black poop. Now, my mom had never had a puppy before, plus I guess she didn't know just exactly how many blueberries I had eaten. When she saw the poop, she said, "Omigosh, Bridget is bleeding internally! She must have eaten something poisonous at the farm!" She scooped up a bag full of poop in one hand and me in the other and rushed me off to the vet.

Needless to say, Dr. Todd had a pretty good laugh about the berry-munching puppy and her hysterical mother.

Of course, I'm much more mature now, which means that when I stand on my hind legs, I can reach the kitchen counter. I also now know that first you scout around the truck for people's lunches, and then you eat the berries for dessert!

Sadie

Dog's Name: **Sadie**
Breed: **Doberman**
Age: **4 years**
Sex: **Female**
Owner: **Victoria Driver**
Location: **Illinois**
Damage: **$5,000**

My mom did a lot of baking this past weekend, and I guess it goes without saying that she came home on Monday after work to a broken plate and a few crumbs on the kitchen floor! Dad told her that he thought about moving the plate before he left but he's just saying that so he won't get in trouble! Anyway, my *most* important caper was really something. I started throwing up on a Saturday, and no one thought too much about it.

But when I hadn't been able to keep even water down by Sunday night, I went to the emergency vet. The vet gave me IVs and I felt a bit better when Mom came to get me before work on Monday morning. The vet insisted that I had to go to the regular vet for the day, so Mom had to drive me all the way across town before work. What a day I had!

When Mom came to get me in the evening, the vet said, "This animal cannot be caged." Well of course I can't! Who wants to sit in a cage?!

He said I have "separation anxiety." All I know is that I like to be next to my human at all times! Since I couldn't be caged, I couldn't stay overnight at the vet.

For the next three days, I didn't keep down any food or water, and Mom had to drive me to the vet every morning for IVs and pick me up every evening.

They made me a "playpen" at the vet by boxing me in a corner (it's not a cage!), and they had a vet tech sit by me all day to keep me company. Boy, did Mom pay through the nose for that.

At night, I came home and slept in the bed with Mom and Dad. Everytime I so much as turned over, they grabbed a bucket and towels 'cause I kept throwing up. I was pretty sick by this time.

The vet had taken every X ray possible and found nothing. They gave me a "barium series"—which I threw up before they could find the problem. That was expensive, too. They recommended exploratory surgery.

The vet showed Mom an X ray and said, "There's one thing here that I can't quite make out." Mom took one look and said, "It's a corncob. She's eaten a corncob."

That corncob was quite tiny, but I guess it was stuck in my small intestine like a cork in a wine bottle. The bill was huge. Mom says it's a good thing she charged it on her L.L. Bean Visa, because she'll probably get a "free" sweater out of the deal.

Remember, all you pups out there, you'll never know if it's edible until you try eating it!

Did YOU Eat the Steaks?

Dog's Name: **Tyler**
Breed: **Cocker Spaniel**
Age: **Puppy**
Sex: **Male**
Owner: **Lynn Rouzer**
Location: **Nelsonville, Ohio**
Damage: **$25**

This story began months ago, and has taken awhile to really "come together." Here goes: About five months ago, my mom bought some really nice steaks at the grocery while with her friend.

As they unpacked the groceries, I watched as A.P. placed the tantalizing steaks into the freezer. As I salivated, no one noticed me. I figured that I would show them!

I knew that if I merely was patient, my moment of satisfaction would come. A few days later, A.P. visited again, and moved the steaks to the fridge, thinking that Mom could make them for supper over the next day or two.

The following morning, Mom grabbed an apple from the fridge on her way out to work. The door to the fridge did not seal! My one shot! I pulled open the door, extracted the steaks and feasted to my heart's content! As I slowly licked my chops after eating I realized that the Styrofoam plate that the steaks were packaged in could be used as evidence against me! Thus, I stashed it between the washer and dryer.

That evening, Mom went to make the steaks. She looked in the freezer. She looked in the refrigerator. She looked up and down, alas, to no avail. Hee! Hee! I heard her pick up the phone, and she called A.P. Here's the conversation:

Mom: Did you take the steaks, A.P.?

A.P.: No, I just put them in the fridge.

Mom: But they aren't there. Are you *sure* you didn't take the steaks?

A.P.: Are you accusing *me?* Maybe it was Sue. She visited the next day.

Mom: OK, I'll ask Sue.

I waited, with bated breath. . .

Mom: Hello Sue, when you were at my house, did you happen to take some steaks? They're missing.

Sue: Why would I steal your steaks? I'm your friend! Are you accusing *me?* Maybe it was Russ. Didn't he house-sit for you the other night?

Mom: OK, I'll ask Russ.

Anyway, you see where this was going. Many folks had the opportunity to "steal" the steaks. Mom summarily asked *each* one, and almost alienated her closest group of friends. I was feeling kind of guilty by now, but I didn't know what to do. I just laid low until a couple a months later.

You can picture what happened . . . Spring cleaning time. Mom moved the washer and found this strange Styrofoam plate with pooch teeth marks in it.

I watched as the realization of *who ate the steaks* fell over Mom's face. She knew it was me . . . Not only did I "steal her supper," but I managed to strain several friendships.

Looking back, I suppose that I'd do things differently—hindsight *is* 20/20. *Next time, I'd hide the Styrofoam plate better!!!*

Nick

Dog's Name: **Nicodemus, or Nick for short**
Breed: **Newfoundland**
Age: **1 year**
Sex: **Male**
Owner: **Betsy Naramore**
Location: **Cincinnati, Ohio**
Damage: **$10**

I'm a Newfoundland, which means I'm pretty big. When I was younger, I liked to pull dishes out of the sink—I was tall enough to do that even then. Well, one night my master made some french fries, with a big ol' kettle of vegetable oil.

So, the next day, he left this (cold) kettle of good-smellin' oil on the stove, and went off to earn green stuff to pay my food bills. So I decided I was gonna try this stuff. Suffice it to say that was not a good idea. Any problems with constipation I may have had before eating that quart or so of vegetable oil went out the door, so to speak. My master came home to find lots of really smelly pools of the remains of my vegetable oil, and me looking up at him the same way he's looked after some weekends. So he let me outside to do my business (again), and boy, I felt really awful for about two days. He sure didn't need to scold me for that little prank; I learned that lesson on my own. I never got any dirty dishes off the stove again.

Ice Cube Retrieval

Nittany

Dog's Name: **Nittany**
Breed: **Labrador Retriever**
Age: **2 years**
Sex: **Female**
Owner: **Christy Smyers**
Location: **Pennsylvania**
Damage: **No Ice-Cold Soda for the Night**

One afternoon, I saw Dad getting ice, which I just love to chew on, out of the door of the fridge. He just walked away without giving me a piece. If this was going to continue, I knew I would have to learn to do it myself.

One day, when Dad wasn't home and Mom was in another room, I thought I would give it a try. I jumped and tried to push the button with my paw. That wasn't working.

Next, I tried pushing it with my nose. It worked! Mom came running out of the other room to see what was going on.

She smiled and said I wasn't really a Bad Dog. She just gets upset when I put my paw prints all over the fridge door.

Edwin

Dog's Name: **Edwin the Destroyer**
Breed: **Dachshund**
Age: **10 years**
Sex: **Male**
Owner: **Holly Deeds**
Location: **Chattanooga, Tennessee**
Damage: **$10**

Sometimes my owner leaves me with my daddy. His house was designed especially for me because it doesn't have *any* doors—not even on cabinets! I can get at anything left at my level without the slightest effort!!

Happily, Daddy hasn't caught on to this and continues to leave food around where I can get it. When I was left there for a couple of weeks while my owner went to London (bad food there, I hear), I discovered a box of my *favorite* food in Daddy's kitchen—*Pop Tarts!!*

My owner only gives me the corners off the Pop Tarts, and *those* I have to share with the other two Dachsies, Katie the Voracious and Lucie the Gentle. This time, though, I got to eat the *whole box*—even the wrappers!

When Daddy called my owner to tell on me, there was a lot of angst in London, but, as usual, my iron constitution had no problem digesting the lot.

The next time my owner left me with Daddy, the kitchen was thoroughly searched before I was left alone—at least they *thought* it was thoroughly searched!

I found cans of some powdered junk called Slim-Fast that I tore into. I even tried to eat a can of shortening, but it wasn't too tasty.

If only Daddy will buy some more Pop Tarts next time I visit, I'll be a very happy Bad Doggy!

Coso

Dog's Name: **Coso**
Breed: **Mix**
Age: **2 years**
Sex: **Male**
Owners: **Holly and Robert Fisher**
Location: **Ridgecrest, California**
Damage: **$250**

I'm Coso, a dog who was abandoned and temporarily adopted by my new mom and dad. They'd like to keep me, but already have three dogs, three cats and two turtles. Well, I've had a very busy past couple of weeks. Let me tell you about them . . .

Mom and Dad were out front digging holes and the other dogs were playing in the backyard. Mom and Dad won't let me hang out with them because Whiz, the other boy dog in the house, doesn't like me very much.

Well, I was lonely and wanted to play, too, so I climbed up on the computer table and hit the window screen a few times. It popped out!

I jumped out of the window and played with the puppy for a while. When Mom and Dad noticed I was out, they got pretty mad, put me back in the room and shut the window.

A couple of days later, Mom and Dad went away and left me alone again, but they didn't leave me outside this time. They put me in the room with the computer where I sleep at night. There's a nice couch there to sleep on and a toilet to get a drink from. I went in to get myself a drink and saw a "window" above the sink. Well, I jumped up on that sink and all of a sudden water started coming out of the tap, so I jumped down. The water was hot, too! After a minute or two, water started pouring over the edges. I guess I must've put the plug in somehow. Mom came home an hour or so later and found water everywhere!

It had been running so long that the water wasn't hot anymore. Four (carpeted) rooms had great big puddles! Mom tried really hard to get the water up, but it still squished between my toes for three or four days.

It smelled pretty bad, too, and Mom and Dad were mad because they couldn't even open the window.

They tried opening it just a little bit, but I was too smart for them and nudged it open with my nose and jumped out. I sure showed them.

They haven't been putting the screen in the window lately. I guess that's because it sort of got broken in two. Mom and Dad were playing on the computer and eating the other night and they had the window open. Chopin, the black cat, jumped out the window and Mom had to go get him. He climbed up a tree and Mom (who is pretty short) just couldn't reach him and called for Dad.

They were outside for about forty-five seconds and when they came back, they found me standing on the table eating Mom's pizza. Boy, were they mad! They yelled just like they did the last five times I ate some of the garbage (and played with the rest).

Boy, I wonder what kind of trouble I can get into next!

Minnie, left; Bob, right

Dog's Name: **Bob**
Breed: **Yorkshire Terrier**
Age: **2 years**
Sex: **Male**
Owner: **Tobi Anderson**
Location: **California**
Damage: **A Tubby Terrier**

This is actually a story about my sister, Minnie, who's only 1¹/₂ and is a little heavier than me. We're big giant Yorkies. I weigh around 13 pounds and she weighs 14 or so. I don't weigh so much because I like the lean look. Also, I don't weigh so much because she is one of the bossiest, meanest, toughest alpha females you would ever hope to meet.

Anyway, Mom and Dad treated her like a little princess and I think they spoiled her. I am generally known as sweet Bob because of my good nature.

One of the reasons I am slim is that she gobbles every little tidbit that comes our way. She will even try to steal Mom and Dad's food.

A couple of weeks ago, Mom was eating her dinner on the couch in front of the TV (a shameful people habit) and Minnie snuck up, reached over her shoulder and snatched a corncob. Mom let her get away with it because there was no corn left on it and Minnie likes to take her stolen booty under Mom and Dad's bed and there is no way that you can get her out of there!

Well, now, Minnie remembered this caper and the yummy reward. (Did she share with me, you ask? Heck, no.) A few nights later, Minnie gave me a look as if to say, "Pay attention, Bob, you might learn something!" as she pulled the same stunt.

Only thing is, Mom was eating a taco. Man, that thing was loaded. Well, all the filling flew out of the taco as Minnie whipped it off the plate. There was lettuce, tomato, corn, beans, avocado, cheese and an awful lot of this red sauce, and it was on Mom's face, in her hair, on the walls, on the couch.

Minnie ran to the bedroom and scuttled under the bed with a big sloppy tortilla. She has her pride and ate it, hot sauce and all. Boy, was Mom shocked. She did look sort of silly sitting there covered with food.

Minnie and I had a good laugh over that one—when Mom and Dad weren't around.

David with Lisa

Ruger

Dogs' Names: **David and Ruger**
Breeds: **Greyhound and German Whitehaired Pointer**
Ages: **6 years and 1 year**
Sex: **Males**
Owners: **Lisa Olson-McDonald and Chris McDonald**
Location: **Cottage Grove, Wisconsin**
Damage: **An Empty Stomach**

One day, my human, Chris, wanted to eat lunch. It was the day before pay-day and the only food in the house (besides our dog food) was a frozen pizza. He cooked the pizza and settled down on the couch to eat it.

We decided that dog food was getting a little too boring, and thought that Chris should share his pizza with us. We first tried looking cute and putting our paws up and begging real nice.

He told us to go away because that was the *only* food in the house until tomorrow. Well, that was not what we wanted to hear. We devised a great plan to get the pizza.

First I, David, ran to the door to be let outside. Chris got up to let me out and Ruger grabbed a slice of pizza. By the time he noticed what happened, Ruger had finished his piece.

Then Ruger went to the door to be let out. Chris let me in, and while he was tying Ruger up, I grabbed my slice of pizza.

Ha ha ha! What a sucker! He fell for the old tag-team routine, and we got our pizza! Very tasty, I might add. Poor Chris had to go without food for the day. We offered him some kibble, but he didn't seem interested.

We've tried this routine many times since, but apparently he has figured it out. Oh well, it worked once.

CHAPTER 5
Doggy-Do

Pongo Bernstein

Dog's Name: **Pongo Bernstein**
Breed: **Mix**
Age: **1 year**
Sex: **Female**
Owners: **Janna Bernstein and Mark Rhodes**
Location: **New York, New York**
Damage: **One Ballerina Slipper**

When I was about a year old, my mom and dad took me to Montreal to visit my grandparents. Everyone was really nice there and called me a "pateet shen."

When Mom and Dad and Grandpa went to the ballet one night, I got to stay home with Grandma and eat pâté and French bread. Then, I found a pair of old ballet shoes and figured that they must be for chewing (isn't everything?).

They were Grandma's shoes—she was a ballerina and she's really strong, carrying me around and all—and she thought it was so cute that I wanted to chew the shoes that she gave them to me.

So I chewed and chewed and chewed. One ballet shoe was totally decimated (Can you tell I was adopted from a shelter in a college town?) by the time we left; I was still chewing the other one in the car on the way back home.

After about eight hours, Mom pulled over for a bathroom break and I got out. I really had to go, so I pulled over to the nearest grass (in front of the windows of the rest stop restaurant) and started to do my business.

Well! That ballet shoe was stringier than I thought it was and I guess I swallowed more than I thought I did, because before I knew it I had a big, stringy, ballet BM hanging out of my butt!

I didn't know what to do, so I started barking at my butt—maybe I could scare it into finishing the job! Mom and Dad were pretty upset, because they didn't realize it was stringy and that I was swallowing some of it—string is very dangerous to eat!

Then I saw all the people in the restaurant looking out the window and pointing and laughing at me. I was really embarrassed, and then I got really mad.

Fortunately, Mommy yelled at Daddy to get her some napkins and he must've run and gotten them while I was busy barking at my butt.

Mom carefully extracted the shoe from my posterior and I was much happier. But I didn't want to be near the people who were laughing at me. So I dragged Mom and Dad back to the car.

I just turned six in March, and I've learned my lesson about shoe-chewing—don't swallow. Just a friendly tip!

Fred Krueger

Dog's Name: **Fred Krueger**
Breed: **German Shepherd mix**
Age: **5 years**
Sex: **Male**
Owner: **Kerry Krueger**
Location: **Pittsburgh, Pennsylvania**
Damage: **$500**

I'm a 6-year-old German Shepherd and "fluffy dog" mix. I came to live with my mom, Kerry Krueger, after I ended up at the shelter during a very loud war (Mom says it was July 4th) when I ran away from my old mom and dad. Kerry let me live in her bedroom when she went to work, and I thought that was pretty cool.

One day, Kerry left me in her bedroom, as usual, with a hook on the outside of the door in case I got adventurous. About halfway through the day, I realized I had to poop *bad!* I'm a really good dog, so going in Mom's bedroom was out of the question.

I tried to get out of the door, but even after I tore part of the frame off the door and scratched big dents in the door, the lock wouldn't budge. I even tried to get through the wall, but just left some really big marks.

All of a sudden, I saw the window. It was open to let the breeze in, so I hiked my big old husky body up on top of my mom's hope chest, leaving some nicely customized claw marks in the top, and I looked out the window.

I figured, gee, if I can get out there, I'll be able to be good and go poop outside! I tore the screen out of the window, and I took a look out the window . . . and I realized it was a three-story drop to the ground . . . whoops!

So, Plan B came to mind . . . I hiked my butt up over the edge of the windowsill, and I let fly with a big old dog poop!

Feeling much better, I retired to the bed for a well-deserved nap. Mom and Dad came home from work, saw all of the "work" I had done during the day and looked really upset.

Then Dad hung his head out the window, to see what I was trying to get out the window for. When he spied the large dump of doggie-doo on the downstairs neighbors' chaise lounge chair, he just laughed.

He told Mom they couldn't be mad about the mess—it was the work of Fred, the smartest dog in the world! That's me!

Jake

Dog's Name: **Jake**
Breed: **Cocker Spaniel**
Age: **5 years**
Sex: **Male**
Owner: **Katie Tarantino**
Location: **Columbia, South Carolina**
Damage: **A Little Doggy Dignity**

My human recently had a new addition to the family. One night, the baby was sitting in his bouncy seat on the floor while the other humans had dinner. When the little human started crying, they noticed that his funny-looking white plastic pants had leaked and took him to the changing table to clean him up.

That was my chance to do a little cleaning up myself! I just could not get over how delicious that brownish residue that had been left behind on the little human's seat was. It was even better than licking the other little human's high chair clean after dinner. I just could not understand why my owner got all upset about it. I was only trying to help!

Dog's Name: **Hodge Podge**
Breed: **Great Dane**
Age: **7 years**
Sex: **Male**
Owner: **Dan Lilly**
Location: **Houston, Texas**
Damage: **Bedding Ruined**

Never in my life would I attempt to voice my displeasure to my manservant. Oh no. That would be wrong (and dangerous, depending on Dan's mood).

When I'm upset, I take it out on Paul. He is a mere servant of a servant, being Dan's underling, and therefore a fair target. My favorite means for letting Dan know I'm upset is, of course, to leave fecal material in strategically located areas.

Paul's bed is the most effective location. Whenever Dan displeases me through ineffective scratching, a lack of walking or, say, going away for the weekend, I just add a touch of my private stock to Paul's sheets.

Being a Dane of 195 pounds makes my royal droppings truly imperial in volume and quality. The missive never goes unnoticed.

During the last such session, I held my bowels for two days before delivering unto the bedding my symbols of malaise.

Most effective indeed!

What I Left on Jennifer's Bed . . .

Sinjun

Dog's Name: **Sinjun**
Breed: **Rottweiler**
Age: **3 years**
Sex: **Female**
Owner: **Angela Dahrling**
Location: **Athens, Georgia**
Damage: **$50**

My name is Sinjun, and I live with my mom and Jennifer, Mom's college roommate. I love Mom and Jennifer lots, and I really like to sleep on Jennifer's bed when she is not home.

Mom doesn't understand why I like Jennifer's bed so much, but I would rather sleep on Mom's bed with Mom, so I sleep on Jen's bed when Mom's not sleeping.

The reason I emphasize my love of Jennifer's bed is to help your humans understand why I did what I did . . . ya'll of course will understand, no problem.

Well, one day, Mom and Jennifer were going to go shopping, and normally I can go too and protect the car—my favorite job because I *love* going for R-I-D-E-S!! (Mom thinks I can't spell, but little does *she* know! Are your humans silly like that, too?)

This day, however, Mom said it was *too hot*. I was very depressed—I mean, can't she leave the car running? It's not like I'm going to let anyone drive off with it (and *me!*) or anything!!

But no, they left me at home. Now, as you all know, doggies are *very smart* and when it comes to expressing our displeasure, we can be very creative and find ways to say exactly what we mean . . . precisely.

So, I thought the best way to let my true feelings on the matter show was to leave Mom and Jen a little present . . . on Jennifer's bed.

So, I did. I was very dainty about it—I left one little piece of poop right in the very center of Jennifer's blanket, then vacated the area.

Now, any of you larger dogs know, as I do, that your humans know very well that you never just poop one little piece. I thought it was very effective—Jennifer *howled* (just like I did when they left me!) and Mom had to buy her a new blanket. (I didn't get my new bone that week because of replacement costs!)

All in all, though, it was worth it because now this is Mom's favorite piece of evidence for my intelligence (to those who doubt our collective canine brilliance, allow me to say "PFFFFT!").

Hope you are inspired by my story—Let 'em know when you're mad! Don't stifle your frustrations! It's not good to bottle things up! Love to all!!

Dog's Name: **Murfee**
Breed: **English Mastiff**
Age: **Puppy**
Sex: **Female**
Owner: **Carol Taylor**
Location: **Toronto, Canada**
Damage: **$5,000**

I was galloping wildly around the backyard, whipping my head from side to side. Every so often, I'd stop and roll around on the grass, gazing dolefully at my rear end. "What is that?"

Puzzled, I ran over to my mom and dad and they said they saw something attached to my butt. Maybe it was a burr or a clump of thistle grass? I raced around the yard some more, very bothered by this foreign object that had attached itself to my rear.

All of a sudden, Mom and Dad were laughing so hard at me! "What's so funny?" I thought.

They saw it was a half-digested Barbie head, dangling from my rear by just the hair. Oops, I remembered eating a Barbie head for snack! What's it doing there? Spooky, to say the least!

I continued to run around the yard and could feel that Barbie head waving in the breeze. My mom and dad debated whether or not they should try and catch me and detach the grisly remnant of my snack. They were both still laughing hard at me. A lot of help they were!

That's when I decided I better cut back on having too many Barbie heads in my diet.

Oh, I've eaten so many things—part of a chair, most of a coffee table, and assorted plastic action figures. Let me tell you about what Mom calls my "most spectacular demolition." I didn't even have to chew on this one! All I needed was my massive natural strength.

I don't tolerate the cold very well, but they still made me go outside to do "my business." I especially hated it when I had to leave a nice, warm fire.

One night, they didn't open the patio doors to let me back in fast enough, so I simply slammed my big body against them once. I was just trying to knock. Hey, I was freezing outside!

I forgot about my strength and smashed the entire pane of glass out of its frame and onto the floor. Well, that was an easy and quick way to get back into the warm house. Then I simply walked over the mess and back to the cozy fireplace. No need to get frantic!

Darby, left; Rascal, right

Dogs' Names: **Rascal and Darby**
Breeds: **Terrier Mix and Australian Shepherd**
Ages: **5 and 6**
Sexes: **Male and Female**
Owner: **Matthew Pritchett**
Location: **Nicholasville, Kentucky**
Damage: **$10 Worth of Dog Shampoo**

The night was dark and rainy. Not at all a good night for being out. I always prefer my bed to any activity anyway, so going out on a night like that was *definitely* not my idea of fun.

My sister, Darby, talked me into it, really. You see, she's an Australian Shepherd, and like most Australian Shepherds, she *thinks* that she's supposed to be a herding dog, even though she really doesn't have a clue about herding. But, I do try to humor her sometimes, because she's so sensitive about it.

So, that night, when she began to fantasize about going over to the nearby farm to herd some cattle, I finally gave in and went along, not realizing how messy the weather was until it was too late.

I, myself, harbor no such false self-image. I know that I'm no herding dog, and actually would be afraid of cattle if they weren't so slow. Being a terrier, I can outrun a cow with no problem, but I'd much rather be chasing a rat or a fox . . . something that doesn't have hard, fast hooves. But, I knew I could get away without any real danger to myself, so, as I said, I agreed to go.

We took off over the hill, over several hills, actually, following my sister's nose. I will give her this: She can definitely smell out the cattle. But, can't anybody? Their smell is really unlike anything else I've come across, and I really don't know how to describe it.

If you've ever been around cows, you know exactly what that smell is. But, Darby seems drawn to it somehow and quickly led us right to the whole bunch of them. We started chasing them and, I must admit, were having a grand old time.

But I knew that she was getting way too serious about this whole thing when she decided that we needed a better "sneak attack." And her way of getting the surprise factor was to make *us* smell like *them!!!*

When she first started making the suggestion, I really didn't believe that she could possibly be serious about this—roll in *that* stuff!!???!!! Yuck, Yuck, Yuck!!! I'm not the neatest little dog around, but I do prefer a nice dog smell to that of a cow pie!

So, at first, I refused to go along. Enough is enough, and running around in the rain seemed like plenty. But, the more I watched her rolling around, squirming and wiggling and covering herself in it, the more it started to look like fun. So I jumped in and joined her.

I think her idea actually worked. Once the cows couldn't smell any dogs around, they settled down much more quickly and we were able to actually sneak up and nip their heels before they even knew we were around.

After we tired ourselves out, reality set in. How were we ever going to face our humans? They always worked so hard to keep us clean! We were so ashamed of the way we looked and smelled, we finally decided not to go home at all—just to stay out in the rain and hope that it would eventually wash that horrible stuff off of us.

Our humans must have been worried about us, because we soon heard them yelling for us from just over the hill. They had driven around for who knows how long, trying to find us. Our glee over hearing their voices overcame our embarrassment, and we ran to the car, ready to jump in and head for home. But, our humans would have nothing of letting us in the car the way we smelled! So, they snapped on our leashes and actually held on to them out the car windows, while they slowly drove back home.

I must admit, I was certainly proud of my human for giving us a bath that night. Of course it was midnight by then, and it wasn't a pretty sight. The water streaming off our bodies was almost black, and you can imagine the smell—that is, if you've ever been around cows!

CHAPTER 6
Flatulence

Weiner Schnitzel

Dog's Name: **Weiner Schnitzel**
Breed: **Dachshund**
Age: **1 year**
Sex: **Male**
Owner: **Kimberly C. Lanum**
Location: **Atlanta, Georgia**
Damage: **Olfactory Discomfort**

My name is Weiner Schnitzel Lanum—W. Schnitzel for short, please. I live in Atlanta, Georgia, with my mom and dad, Kim and David.

Anyway, Mom has been getting a little frustrated with me lately because, you see, I have this little problem: *Gas*. It's been so bad lately that Mom has had to leave my presence, roll down a window or turn on the ceiling fan, whatever works.

Mom, Dad and I were in the car one day, going to the grocery store, when suddenly Mom nearly swerved off the road! I was very comfortable sitting in Dad's lap, so it really startled me.

She said to Dad, "Did you do that?" Dad doesn't smell so well so he said, "What?"—and then it hit him.

They started rolling down the car windows as fast as they could. Mom said she was about to suffocate and that something was going to have to be done about my problem.

We returned home that evening and I got up into Mom's lap while she was sitting on the couch. I was so tired that I turned over onto my back (my favorite sleeping position) and went to sleep.

I suppose some time passed, but suddenly Mom picked me up and put me on the floor. She seemed to be in a tizzy about something! She kept saying "Schnitzel, *what* is *wrong* with *you!?*"

I just looked at her as I was waking up. She turned on the ceiling fan and left me in the room by myself. So I guess I have a little problem with passing bad gas.

If anybody has a solution, please let us know. Mom gives me a look now that sort of says, "Don't you dare." But I just can't help it.

Benchley with feline friend

Dog's Name: **Benchley**
Breed: **Mix**
Age: **1 year**
Sex: **Male**
Owners: **Jay and Diana**
Location: **New York, New York**
Damage: **A Brush with the Paranormal**

I'm Benchley, and I'm just over a year old. My mom and dad adopted me from the ASPCA. I now live with them and my cat brother, Muff, in Washington Heights, which is really cool because we are surrounded by parks, and me and my doggie friends meet everyday to play.

I love life! I love to meet new people, kids and, especially, dogs. I'm basically pretty fearless, and pretty smart, well, but, uh, can I confide in you? There's something peculiar going on . . . a sort of mystery, and, well, I haven't been able to figure this out, and, frankly, it's starting to freak me out.

You see, there's this thing, it attacks me every once in a while. I haven't actually caught what's doing it, but, sometimes, when I'm just standing there, minding my own business, something grabs my butt, shakes it and leaves a smelly odor behind.

I've tried turning around really quickly to see if I can catch it, but I've never been able to. It even gets me when I'm sitting! I turn around, don't see anyone and I then smell the ground, and sure enough, there's that stinky smell that always scares my brother, Muff, out of the room.

To be honest, it scares me too; it's like it disappears into the ground. I look around, check my butt again and then run away into the bedroom. Mom and Dad try to comfort me, but I don't think they can see the fart monster either.

Once, it even got me in the park. I was just standing, surveying one of my favorite greens, when, pow! It even made a loud noise! I turned around quickly, looked around, smelled my butt, turned around again and saw a big, bushy boxwood it must have run into. I ran to it, looked and sniffed around to see if I could catch its scent, to no avail. I turned around just to see Mom and Dad, of all things, laughing.

What is going *on* here? If you know anything, or have ever seen this elusive fart monster, *please* let me know. Maybe we can catch it together.

Sirius, the Dog Star

Dog's Name: **Idgie**
Breed: **German Ridgeback?**
Age: **4 years**
Sex: **Female**
Owner: **Dr. Hu**
Location: **San Francisco, California**
Damage: **One Broken Golden Rule**

I'm a blend of Rhodesian Ridgeback and German Shepherd. I am particularly handsome because I have a prominent, inch-high ridge along my back. Very punk. The boys like me. Humans think my hackles are up, so they respect me.

I don't act like a Shepherd. Obedience training pitted my houndness against my mom's Ph.D. in psychology. She didn't really win. Sure I do the commands, but I do them *my* way.

Well, after I finally graduated from obedience class, my mom took me to college. She teaches psychology and I'm the Teaching Assistant during the lecture about Operant Conditioning.

It's a little boring for me because she goes on and on about stuff I heard last semester, but it involves *treats*. Mom calls it "positive reinforcement," but it tastes swell anyway. She uses special treats because she really wants the demonstration to work, so she hunts hot dogs the week before, and brings tiny bits of them to class for me!

The night before class, I found a whole stash of hot dog treats and gobbled them up. Of course, the blame went to my sister, Rocket, who is the Naughty Dog (I am the Good Dog).

But the next day, my mom found out who really ate the treats, because I had farts in class. Powerful farts. Praise to Sirius, the dog star, the flaming ball of gases lighting the skies!

The whole front row of students passed out. The rest of the students were making faces and fanning their hands during the whole lecture. My mom was embarrassed, even though she's not the one who farted, and farts are nothing to be ashamed of anyway. Especially these farts—they were magnificent!

Finally, class ended. The students didn't want the next group of students to think that one of *them* had farted, so they made Mom write on the chalkboard, "The *dog* farted. Sorry." I think most fart stories are sophomoric, but this was actually with freshmen/freshwomen.

CHAPTER 7
In the Yard

Booker

Dog's Name: **Booker**
Breed: **Mix**
Age: **1 year**
Sex: **Male**
Owner: **Steve Hochfelsen**
Location: **California**
Damage: **$25**

My sister Keik and I are really lucky. We get our run of the house and have a good doggie door so we can go out in the yard and play, too!

We also have lots of friends who love to come play with us. Shasta, the Husky in the back, is a little neurotic, but she's a real party animal, if you know what I mean.

Once in awhile, Keik and I will dig a little hole under the fence so Shasta can lick us through the hole. The holes are not usually very big—only about two or three feet deep, and a couple of feet wide.

Shasta helps by doing the same thing on the other side, so she can fit her whole head, up to her chest, under the fence. Then we play the growl, bark and lick game.

Sometimes Keik gets carried away, and barks nonstop for 20 minutes or so, until the neighbors start to complain. Then, on the side, we have Scout. Scout is a great big German Shepherd, and he has real digging skills. In fact, one day, through a major team effort, we decided to let Scout come and visit us under the fence.

After he got into our yard, we showed him how to use our real fun doggie door. He thought it was really neat, because he was able to mark his territory both inside and outside our house with impunity.

I don't understand why he felt the need to do it eight times on the living room carpet, but he said it was necessary. Oh, well.

I did, however, draw the line when he opened the refrigerator and ate last night's pot roast off the bottom shelf, plastic wrap and all. I decided I should help out on that one.

Dad didn't seem to mind. He seemed more amused than mad when he opened the front door to our house and was greeted by three, rather than two, dogs. He seemed a little more irked when he realized that most of the food in the refrigerator had spoiled and his dinner for that night was gone.

Keik was sure we had done something wrong and immediately peed all over herself. But, hey? What do you want when you leave us home alone all day?

A dog's gotta have *some* fun!!

Does Metal Have Any Nutritional Value?

Coney (center)

Dog's Name: **Coney**
Breed: **Akita**
Age: **9 years**
Sex: **Male**
Owners: **The McNeely Family**
Location: **Tallahassee, Florida**
Damage: **$5,000**

My name used to be Kokomo and then Beast, because I can act like one, but for the last seven years it has been Coney because my ears fold across my head in the shape of a large cone.

My destructive *pièce de résistance* occurred this past summer. After the annual Tallahassee thunderstorm season began, it became obvious that I could not be left alone in the house because when my folks were out I'd scratch open every closet door and throw all of the shoes and things across each room.

Then I'd stand on the beds and try to dig a hole into the mattresses, just in case I might be able to hide in the hole (rather than just climbing under the bed, which is too easy for someone like me, who likes a challenge).

So, my folks forked over several hundreds of dollars to build me a kennel with a thick chain-link fence and a sunroof so that I would be comfy, yet unable to escape and roam the neighborhood looking for the trash man or the UPS deliverer (my archenemies).

Well, within a week I had chewed not one, but two holes through the chain fence, wearing down most of my teeth. My folks then tied me to a wire rope inside the kennel, away from the two holes. But I really like my freedom!

I chewed a third hole through the fence, which I strategically positioned so that I could climb out and still have enough rope length to reach the side of the brand-new metal yard building that my folks had just spent a week installing. It was an expensive Arrow model.

With my remaining teeth I managed to chew a hole through the corner of the yard building, then I reached in and pulled out an upright floor buffer (they didn't need it anyway; I've already destroyed the wood floor), two tents (one of which I decided to chew a hole in, just for fun—it wasn't much of a challenge after the metal fence and building), a leaf blower, miscellaneous garden tools and a weed wacker.

Then I climbed in, gleefully waiting for them to come home and witness my handiwork! Mom was so shocked, she simply turned around and walked back into the house without saying a word. But Dad sure had a few choice words to say when he got home. The next day, I had my very own prescription for valium!

Besides these "slight problems," I am a loving and loyal member of the family. I get special treats at the vet when I board because I am so "well-behaved." I've also helped to raise four kids who love to take me for walks. But I just can't help losing control of myself when I'm home without them.

Sebastian (front)

Dog's Name: **Sebastian**
Breed: **Mastiff**
Age: **3 years**
Sex: **Male**
Owners: **Clifford and Tiffany Brady**
Location: **Hillsboro, Oregon**
Damage: **$500**

I am a very handsome 180-pound Mastiff. I take very good care of three little boys whom I love with all my huge heart.

We just bought a brand-new house and my master spent all last summer and about $3,000 installing our backyard for me to play in.

Well, I greatly appreciated the lawn, but had no idea why anyone would feel that shrubs and lighting were necessary! The lights get in the way of running through the yard and the shrubs, aside from targets for peeing on, are pretty useless. Sooooo, I decided to remove them—*all* of them.

First, I chewed that really expensive tree that took years for someone to train to grow in an "S" curve. It was so curvy, it was too hard to pee on and hit accurately.

Then, I pulled out all the rest of the shrubs. The lights were next—these were tougher, though, because my master had dropped all of the wiring down in the sprinkler trenches before backfilling. I had to actually break all the fixtures in order to pull them out and march past the breakfast window with one in my mouth.

This, however, was a very dramatic and creative way to show my master my handiwork. Well, he wasn't real happy about it and is now committed to finishing my dog run. Yeah, like that'll hold me in!

Cat, left; Poochy, right

Dog's Name: **Poochy**
Breed: **Mix**
Age: **3 years**
Sex: **Female**
Owner: **Antonia K. Clark**
Location: **California**
Damage: **Rain and a Hot Tin Woof**

My master has two cats in addition to me. They never want to play with me. I don't understand why. My master put a long ladder up against a shed in the yard so that the cats could get away from me if I bothered them too much.

One day, I really wanted to play. As usual, the cats did not cooperate. They ran up the ladder to get away from me, but this time I managed to get up the ladder also. Problem . . . I could not figure out how to get down once I got up there.

After work, my master came home. She opened the backdoor expecting me to greet her. She peered around the yard with a puzzled look on her face and finally looked up.

There I was on the shed's roof. Boy, was I glad when she finally rescued me. I had been up there for hours.

You'd think I would have learned the first time, but nooo . . . The next time it was worse—it started raining. I walked on the roof and along the neighbor's narrow fence for two hours waiting for my master to come home.

Finally, the neighbor got a ladder and got me down. She had two dogs and I got to play with them (after the rain stopped) in the backyard. It was fun!

Later she took me to my master's house. My master was just getting home from work. When my master got out of her car, the neighbor approached her and asked if she had lost her dog.

My master said, "Has she been walking on the roof again?" The neighbor told her the whole sordid story.

When my master related the episode to one of her fellow employees, he told her about how they keep dogs on roofs in Mexico as watch dogs. So that is how I became labeled as a Mexican Woof Dog.

P.S. My master moved the ladder.

Poi

Dog's Name: **Poi**
Breed: **Mix**
Age: **Puppy**
Sex: **Female**
Owners: **Patrick and Sherri Wheeler**
Location: **Carlsbad, California**
Damage: **$25**

My owners, Sheri and Pat, like to entertain, and especially they like to bar-becue when the weather is nice. One evening, Pat was barbecuing fish.

After Pat had put the fish on the grill, there was some "fish juice" left in the pan. Well, Pat remembered his good elementary school stories about the Pilgrims learning to plant a fish with their corn, so he figured that a little fish juice could only be good for the health of our lawn. Naturally, he spread it over a good-sized patch.

Well, I had been learning to do a little digging. I'd mostly stuck to soft soil before then, but I had never encountered dirt that smelled *so* promising.

As soon as I found this wonderful smell, I started digging up the whole appetizing section. I didn't find the treat that must have been buried there, but I didn't give up hope.

After my owners (who were not very playful with a puppy as cute as me that day) finished filling the hole, I went ahead and resumed my excavation efforts. They tried covering it with new sod and mixing red pepper into the soil, but I wasn't deterred. I didn't give up on that spot for almost a year.

Pat hasn't repeated his organic fertilizing efforts, though.

Sheena

Dog's Name: **Sheena**
Breed: **Australian Cattle Dog**
Age: **7 years**
Sex: **Female**
Owner: **David Wunderlich**
Location: **Phoenix, Arizona**
Damage: **$600**

Greetings from Arizona! I like to think of things that I can do to help out my owner, Dave, while he is at work.

Being an Australian Cattle Dog, I love the outdoors and landscaping is my calling. Dave's yard wasn't much at first (in fact, it was pretty boring), but I have a great yard now.

First of all, Phoenix is in the middle of the desert, so water is pretty scarce. Most yards consist of a small section of grass surrounded by rock and drought/heat-tolerant trees and plants.

When Dave brought me home, his backyard landscaping consisted of a single three-foot pine tree and dirt. Lots 'n' lots of dirt! I loved dirt as a puppy and I especially enjoyed a good romp in the mud (still do, much to Dave's dismay), so you can imagine my disappointment when Dave planted grass and laid rock in my dirt. I didn't mind the grass so much (it felt nice and cool on my tummy), but I couldn't stand the rock (I wanted my dirt back) and he planted trees and shrubs in all of my favorite places.

As if things weren't bad enough, most of the plants he had chosen were "water hogs" and not on the Phoenix Water Department's good plant list. Drastic measures needed to be taken. Not only had he ruined my dirt, he was going to use up everyone's water!

For the benefit of all living things, I unselfishly decided that getting my dirt back could wait until after I had removed these offensive water-hungry plants.

The first plant I tackled was that stupid pine tree (who ever heard of planting a pine tree in the middle of the desert?). It didn't take long to dig it up and drag it to the side of the house, and I must say that I did enjoy playing in the mud for a little while (all work and no play . . .).

I continued my work by eating two vines (mighty tasty), ripping up numerous hedges (again stopping to play in the mud) and several flowering plants (these would have just attracted bees and bugs anyway).

I had just started the task of removing the rocks from my dirt when Dave got home from work. I met him at the patio door and what can I say . . . he was absolutely speechless. He just stood there admiring my work.

I was all set to accept his bountiful praises when he grabbed me by the collar and dragged me into the garage while muttering several phrases under his breath (that's gratitude for you).

He was extremely mad (guess he took my work as an insult to his "grand plan" . . . the male ego is a sensitive thing) and I was banished to my room for the rest of the evening (well, at least until he couldn't stand listening to me whine anymore).

Well, the next morning I was determined to get my dirt back (I always finish what I start) and I jumped right into the task. Do you know how hard it is to move nine tons of rock?

It took Dave an entire weekend, and I think that it may have taken me a couple of weeks had I not conceived a plan. My plan involved using water (under pressure of course) to move the rocks out of my dirt. This plan had the added benefit of creating mud, which I could play in for the rest of the day. But where would I get the water?

I had remembered seeing Dave use a big green snake to water his grass and sure enough, I found it. It had this metal thing on the end of it and quite by accident I discovered that a very powerful stream of water would come out if I turned it clockwise. I immediately set to work and was very impressed with my success.

Dave came home early that day. (I think one of the neighbors called him. I guess some of the water was seeping into his yard and into the street [wasting water can carry a hefty fine in Phoenix, as we found out].) He was once again speechless.

I couldn't go out in the backyard for two days (it took awhile to dry out and what a punishment . . . all that mud within paw's reach).

Dave and I have slowly but surely redone the backyard. I now have a 15-square-foot area of dirt and he has his precious rock, grass, citrus trees and plants (all of which are on the Phoenix Water Department's good plant list). You can imagine my feelings when Dave decided to plant a vegetable garden using half of my dirt patch.

There were no negotiations or compensation. He just took half of my dirt, half of the area he gave me so I wouldn't dig up the rest of his yard. I'm told that countries go to war over such invasions.

Not only did he take my dirt, but he put a four-foot wood fence around it too. It was like having the Berlin Wall right in my own patch of dirt. This simply would not do.

My first plan of attack was simple enough: Dig under the fence, pull out all of the green beans, tomato plants, etc. and proceed to just frolic in the dirt. What a fun-filled day.

Well, the fun ended when Dave got home. I was once again banished to the garage, but I was tired anyway. It's a lot of work and a lot of play reclaiming my dirt. I just slept on the mat.

The next weekend, Dave took down the fence and I marched triumphantly around the yard. Victory was mine (or so I thought). Dave came home later that afternoon with something called a ditch digger and dug a two-foot-deep trench around his old vegetable garden.

Something was definitely up. Would you believe that he built a cinder-block wall four feet high (with an additional two feet underground)? Now it *really* looked like the Berlin Wall!

To make matters worse, he taunted me by saying, "Let's see you get in there now." Those were fighting words.

It took me a while (three weeks and numerous attempts, resulting in injured paws and nose), but I finally figured out how to get into that garden. A bucket turned upside down makes a darn good stepping stool, and there I stood in the garden.

Time to get to work on reclaiming my dirt! I carefully chose my first victim, bit into it and *yummy!* This plant was a lot tastier than any I had ever destroyed before and I figured out that the tasty part was this red bulb thing.

I found out later that it was a strawberry and I have loved them ever since. Well, I tried a few more and decided that I should probably try out some of the other delicacies. Maybe this garden thing wasn't so bad after all?

I ate a few round things. I think they are called tomatoes. I ate a few green things (beans?) and dug up a few things called radishes (didn't like them at all), and then I came to a bunch of really small plants that smelled really, really good (this was Dave's herb garden).

A word to the wise to all of you puppies who are planning to feast in the garden: Please beware of things called chilies or hot peppers! They are extremely hot and burn just as much coming out as they do in your mouth!

Gasp! I had to get water, but I was trapped. I couldn't jump out of the garden (there was no bucket in sight . . . guess I didn't plan my escape very well) and it felt like I had swallowed a burning match.

Then it hit me. Drip system! I immediately started digging, but there was no pipe to be found (Yikes!) Then I noticed the faucet Dave installed in the corner. Now, I am usually an expert at turning these things on, but my mouth was on fire and I was panicking and I just couldn't get the darn thing on! What was I going to do? Well, luckily the faucet was high enough above the ground to allow me to use it as a step. I was finally free and drinking like a fish at my water bowl.

Dave came home and, as usual, inspected the garden. I was all ready to go to the garage when Dave muttered something about bugs, birds and cats munching on his veggies. He should have known that it wasn't a cat or bird.

I am a dog, after all, and wouldn't let one of those things in my dirt. I just sat by the door and grinned. In fact, I grinned all evening. He thought it was bugs and cats. Ha! I was home free and could dine on strawberries (*yum!*) and tomatoes to my heart's content.

Well, smiling all evening until I got really sick from eating those hot pepper things. I was so miserable and Dave figured out why.

Now I help Dave garden and he always gives me a few strawberries or a tomato or two. That's the deal we made for using part of my dirt.

CHAPTER 8
Confinement

Left to right:
Scarlet,
Cherry,
Preston,
Sherlock

Fawn (insisted on her own "glam" shot)

Dog's Name: **Sherlock**
Breed: **Siberian Husky**
Age: **Puppy**
Sex: **Male**
Owner: **Marilyn K. Waterston, Esq.**
Location: **St. Louis, Missouri**
Damage: **$1,000**

My name is Sherlock. My human kept most of my brothers and sisters, and at 5 months of age, the five of us had a great time. My human had a "dog proof" room in the basement for us.

However, there was a garden hose sticking out underneath the door to the laundry room. Since Mom had gone to work, and we had nothing to do, I believe it was Preston who pulled on the hose. Cherry helped. That forced the door open. Scarlet and Fawn ran into the room first. *Where to start??*

Let me tell you, we had fun. We took all the clothes out of the baskets, and spread them on the floor. We moved the washing machine out from the wall . . . about five feet. Cherry got a broom and ran around with it sticking up in the air, and broke all the light bulbs. This added broken glass to the clothes on the floor. We also found a bag of potting soil; we made sure it was spread evenly across the floor.

Mom had a 270-gallon fish tank in that room with only one very valuable fish in it. Cherry jumped in and went for a swim, and scared the fish so badly he had a heart attack and went belly up. (At least we didn't eat him.) We splashed a lot of the water out of the tank . . . It mixed well with the potting soil, glass and clothes on the floor.

We pulled on the hose, and we almost pulled the pipe out of the wall. We managed to turn the water on, which was still running when Mom got home.

This mixed the potting soil and glass into the clothes on the floor. We tried to pull the copper pipe off the water heater, but just didn't get that job completed. Cherry did pull all the bristles out of the broom, and they mixed with the clothes, dirt . . . You get the picture.

Then we emptied the trash. That was a lay up. The most fun was the dryer lint that was in the trash. We ripped that all apart, and spread it everywhere.

The door must have swung shut behind us, and because we were trapped, we decided to take drastic measures to get out. Preston dug through the drywall. He got most of the way through. But the rest of us chewed on the door, removed a large section of it and managed to get free.

When Mom came home, we were all sitting in the dog room like little angels. The missing part of the door gave us away, though. Mom didn't even say anything when she went into the laundry room.

Later, I heard her say something about being *speechless*. We just woo-wooed at her, and wagged our fuzzy butts. We were not really *bad* dogs . . . I mean, other than the fish, no one got hurt, even with all that glass.

Mom took pictures, because she said no one would believe her. Now every time someone talks to her about getting a Siberian puppy, she shows the photos. How embarrassing!

Jack, left; Bill, right

Dog's Name: **Jack**
Breed: **German Shepherd**
Age: **6 months**
Sex: **Male**
Owners: **Bonnie Guess and Jerry Morris**
Location: **Florida**
Damage: **$250**

When I was only 6 months old, Mom, Dad, me and my older brother Bill were coming back from the Florida Keys and stopped at this motel to spend the night. Hey, it was *sooooo* cool.

I had two big beds to bounce back and forth on while I watched Scooby Doo on TV.

Well, anyway, Mom and Dad went out to dinner. They left Bill and me in the room 'cause they said it was too hot for us to wait in the truck.

Boy! Talk about being @#@#@# off! I thought they needed to know real quick who the boss was from now on. So, right after they left, I began my task. I chewed up Dad's beer carton. Then I ripped the Kleenex holder out of the wall.

I thought I would rest for a while on the bed, but I couldn't sleep, so I started digging. I dug and dug until I had the sheets in shreds. When I got down to the mattress, I wanted to see how it tasted, so I took a few bites out of it. Yuck! Not too tasty. That made me even madder, so I tugged and tugged till I got the mattress off the bed.

All this time my big brother was sitting there just shaking his head saying, "Man are you gonna be in big trouble."

When Mom and Dad got back, Mom thought somebody broke in and vandalized the room. Dad, being the clever fellow he is, knew right away it was me.

It was so funny watching them clean up my mess. They had to flip the mattress over to hide the hole that I made. Then Dad found an unattended maid's cart and "borrowed" some new sheets to put on the bed.

Golly, I still can't figure out why they stuffed the shredded sheets into the suitcase to take home with us.

I guess they really love me 'cause I'm still around. Mom tells me sometimes to go play in traffic, but I know she's just kidding because I've tried it before and I thought she was gonna have a heart attack.

Rupert

Dog's Name: **Rupert**
Breed: **Lab Mix**
Age: **Puppy**
Sex: **Male**
Owner: **Jodi Naas**
Location: **Seattle, Washington**
Damage: **$50**

When I was just a pup, my mom, the dog lover, and her sister, the dog disliker, lived together in a nice white house with a picket fence and a yard with a little gate in the back. I loved that gate because it was my special gateway to freedom. People who think about dogs, like my mom, always close gates. People who don't think about dogs, like my aunt, leave them open. Many a sibling argument was started over this.

Anyway, if Mom didn't notice that the back gate was open, or if it wasn't shut real tight, I'd slip out and roam the neighborhood. Mom always noticed and called me back within a couple of minutes, except one night during a dinner party she was giving for some friends who didn't like dogs very much.

Of course, I was outside, given my propensity to jump up on people's laps, and lo and behold I found the magic gate open that night! I ran out into the wide world, and when Mom came out to find me an hour or so later, I was gone, gone, gone. I'd escaped a couple of times before, but I was always hanging about in the back alley or visiting the pet food store across the street, which had been closed for hours.

Poor Mom was so worried she didn't sleep all night. She kept listening for the tinkling of my collar tags at the back door, she went out and called for me over and over, she called animal control and she cried and cried!

Mom took the next day off from work to look for me, because I'm as important as any child, and much prettier and cleaner.

Around 10 a.m., Mom saw some ladies loading me into a truck! She recognized me immediately. She went racing across the street, screaming, "My dog! That's my dog!"

Well, the ladies were taken aback, and they handed the leash over to Mom on the condition that she pay $35. They handed her a bag of half-chewed toys and told the story.

Seems in the night an employee of the pet store had been working late. The pet store had a back door for deliveries and this had been left open. I sneaked in, hid among the great piles of dog food bags and was locked into the storeroom overnight. The ladies found me chomping on toys in the back room in the morning.

You can only guess how much fun that was for me. And I tried to stick to chewing on the cheap stuff.

Cheyenne Louise, left; Tillie, right

Dog's Name: **Cheyenne Louise**
Breed: **Rottweiler**
Age: **2 years**
Sex: **Female**
Owner: **Meg Buchner**
Location: **Ferryville, Wisconsin**
Damage: **$50**

My name is Cheyenne Louise and I am a Rottweiler. I have a little sister named Tillie who is a Basset Hound. Since she's only 1 and I'm 2, I try to teach her lots of stuff. Recently, I taught her a fun game called "escape." We play it all day long when Mom and Dad are at work.

You see, during the day, Tillie and I stay in our own "house," which is downstairs. We've got our own doggie door to go outside, toys and our bed, but there's lots more fun stuff to play with *outside* our house.

First, Dad built a wooden gate across to keep us in. It wasn't much of a challenge. I would back way up and run at it and jump right over. The latch was on the outside, so I'd just nudge that with my nose and let Tillie out. Then we'd go upstairs and play.

One day, Mom had lots of nice clean laundry folded on top of the dryer. I knocked some off so we could play tug-of-war. Those clothes ripped pretty easily, so we had to move from sweatshirts to blue jeans.

Pretty soon, Dad came home and got out all his tools and took our nice wooden gate right off. He put up a metal chain-link gate, just like our outside fence. It was so high, I couldn't even jump over it.

Tillie and I spent *a week* planning a way to escape this new gate. We tried head-butting it, but it only bent a bit. Then Tillie started poking her pointed little nose through the holes and stretching them out. Next, I'd head-butt them, and she'd stretch them.

Pretty soon we had a little hole in the chain-link gate. It was just big enough for Tillie to squeeze through. Being a short little Basset, she couldn't reach the latch to let me out. It's not much fun to play alone, so Tillie ran and got a pair of Daddy's new work boots. She brought us each one to chew on. Til's a pretty generous little sister.

Mom and Dad got home and Daddy said, "Holy Spit!" Then Mother took us upstairs because we're too young to hear strong language. After Daddy stopped yelling, he got out his welder and fixed the gate. He made it *really* strong and said that would fix us. Dad is really nice; he likes to make our "escape" game quite a challenge.

The next day, I decided I would try throwing myself against the door again. This time, I got the hinges to spring free, even though the latch stayed put. Tillie and I ran right upstairs and pulled some of the books out of the bookcase to chew up.

The next Saturday, Dad went to the store and got lots of lumber. He got out all his tools again and built a picket-fence gate. We've had that for two weeks now and it's really hard to get open. But that's okay, because Tillie thought up a new game called "chew up the bed," which is a lot of fun!

The Great Escape

Dog's Name: **Woody**
Breed: **Mix**
Age: **3 years**
Sex: **Male**
Owners: **Ken and Vesta Armstrong**
Location: **Mount Shasta, California**
Damage: **$10,000**

I like TV and digging. My owners only like TV. I saw a great movie about digging, *The Great Escape*. I decided to dig my way out of our yard.

There is (I should say *was*) a fence four feet high around our yard. There were four-by-four-inch posts supporting it. I dug down just like I saw on TV, but there was a post in the way. So, I moved over a couple of inches and, pretty soon, the area around the post (actually, *all* the posts) holding up the fence was exposed.

I could get out through any number of tunnels. Cool! Just like the movie. I could get out anytime I wanted.

I thought my owners would be pleased with my creativity and perseverance. Boy, was I wrong. Soon after I completed my tunnels, the biggest wind in 50 years (more than 120 mph) blew through the area. The fence blew down and into the neighbor's property. Their fiberglass greenhouse was reduced to rubble.

The next fence required concrete footings because I had softened up the land so much. This is a chain-link type fence. No problem! I can dig out anywhere there isn't a fence post, which is *almost* everywhere. My owners like the game, though, because they keep putting concrete blocks around the fence to make it more interesting. I like it. I keep winning the game.

I have taught Eileen, my dog friend, how to dig in and out, too! So far, they haven't figured out how to keep us in. They like spending money on fencing materials, I think.

Now they're talking about pouring a concrete slab. I'm sure I'll figure a way out of there, too! Happy Digging!

Dog's CAN Fly

Dog's Name: **Teddybearosaurus Rex**
Breed: **Rottweiler**
Age: **1 year**
Sex: **Female**
Owner: **Robert A. Bochicchio**
Location: **Raised Ranch**
Damage: **$25**

I'm Teddybearosuarus Rex, but my family just calls me Bear. I love my family, especially the little blonde girl they call Hannah.

Well, anyway, I was sitting by the upstairs window watching Daddy work out in the front yard. I was also waiting for Hannah to get off the big yellow bus thing, when a strange dog came walking down the street.

He was cute, but he said some terrible things to Daddy and I just had to get outside to keep him from getting nasty. I looked around, but there was no one to let me out of the house.

I yelled to Daddy to open the door, but he was busy, so I jumped out of the window. The window was open, but the screen was not.

I did it just right, too—I pushed with my paws just as I left the floor, and that stupid old screen just tore right out.

I must have landed about 15 feet from the house, 'cause when I hit the ground it made me yelp, but I just rolled head over nub, and didn't even slow down.

I ran right up to the edge of the road and yelled at the nasty dog, but he had already run away. When Daddy ran up to me, I couldn't tell if he was glad or mad, so I gave him my paw.

He sat down and hugged me and asked if I was all right. Then he saw the screen. I got to go for a ride to the screen place to get the screen fixed. Dad said we better do that before Mommy got home. When we got home, Daddy put the new screen in, gave me a cookie and went back to work out front.

That's when Hannah got off the big yellow bus thing. I was so happy, I jumped out the window to go see her. This time the screen landed on the roses.

Daddy put a couch in front of the window for me to sit on while I wait for Hannah, but it's in the way of my favorite doggy door.

I'm a good dog, really I am, and I still don't know what all the fuss was about—I was just doing my job.

CHAPTER 9

Cars

Ronnie

Dog's Name: **Ronnie**
Breed: **Mix**
Age: **3 years**
Sex: **Female**
Owner: **Shari**
Location: **Germantown, Maryland**
Damage: **$2,500**

My owner and I were on our way to a Memorial Day block party when we detoured to a beverage store to pick up some refreshments. I stayed in the car while she went inside.

When my owner returned, beverages in hand, she was baffled to find her car, and me, missing. "Who would steal a car with a canine?" she thought.

Then, in the distance, she saw a crowd gathering near a gas station. As she began running toward the commotion, someone yelled at her, "Lady, get down here. Your dog is scared to death!"

She arrived to find her car wedged underneath a tow truck, with me cowering (okay, I was nervous), under the steering wheel. After she coaxed me out of the car, I explained that I'd accidentally dislodged the parking brake, causing the car to roll out of control until it met its match in the tow truck.

There is a silver lining in this cloud, though. If the car had continued in its path unchecked by the truck, it would have careened directly into a gas pump—I'd have been doggie toast!

At least I lived to tell the tale, despite the damage to my owner's wallet!

Dog's Name: **Bru**
Breed: **Borzoi**
Age: **Puppy**
Sex: **Male**
Owner: **Heather Henson**
Location: **Jewett City, Connecticut**
Damage: **$1,000**

My mom had just bought her brand-new pickup truck and she was so proud! Then, she adopted me to ride around with her and it was great, but I forgot to tell her that I cannot stand to be alone in the car! I want to follow her everywhere!

We stopped at the store and Mommy ran in to do some shopping. "It's nighttime and cool. You'll be fine; I'll only be a few minutes." A few minutes is *too long!* How could she!?!

I felt my stomach get upset and then I had an accident all over the seat. I started jumping all around to try to get Mommy's attention, but she didn't see me. The doo-doo was all over my feet and the seat and the dashboard and the windows, so now I couldn't see the store very well.

This made me more nervous, so I started to chew on the armrest. When that was gone, I chewed the seat up. When the side of the seat was gone, I chewed the visor up. She still was not back! It was almost 10 minutes!! How could she lie!

While I was trying to figure out how to drive into the store, I accidentally chewed the cruise control unit out of the steering wheel.

Then Mommy finally came back. I was so happy to see her, I jumped all over her, but she did not seem happy to see me! I don't know why, but she just started to cry!

When we finally started to ride again (after she put some paper on the seats), a nice police officer pulled us over because Mommy was swerving due to the cruise control thingy that kept falling in her lap.

When the officer looked in the car and at Mom, he just said, "Oh, I'm so sorry," and he let us go!

So my story has a happy ending!

Dog's Name: **Rita**
Breed: **Airedale Terrier**
Age: **Puppy**
Sex: **Female**
Owner: **Gena Ferrari**
Location: **Chattanooga, Tennessee**
Damage: **$1,000**

When I came into Mom's life, she was driving a 1995 white Subaru Legacy wagon with velour seats—as classy as a wagon can be.

I had the whole back end to play in, and usually had a toy or two for my amusement. That was not good enough! I liked the texture of the nylon seat belts in the back!!!

Mom tried using Bitter Apple and other products to discourage me from gnawing on them, to no avail. I had chewed almost through the right-hand one. She tied a knot in it and hid the evidence. At that point, the left one was hanging in, barely. Mom hoped Daddy wouldn't notice. What he *did* notice was the gaping hole in the wheel-well cover. I had been standing on it when it cracked. I can't *stand* ragged edges, and I tried desperately to file it down smooth with my teeth—resulting in about an 8-inch crater that went straight to the wheel.

Then, the car got wrecked. A guy in a van turned in front of my mom—nothing she could do about it. She went to see the car afterward and it looked pretty nasty. She saw her chance—she asked the people at the body shop to find out how much replacing the seat belts would cost and if they would do it "on the sly" while they had the car apart. *"Man o man!!!"* Mom said, "It was $235 *per* seatbelt!" (plus installation, of course). The fiberglass wheel-well cover assembly was about 600 buckeroonies!

After that, she was rooting even harder for a "total loss," and her wish came true. Immediately, she went and bought me a Subaru Outback wagon, with more headroom and more dog-resistant upholstery. I have limited my destructive tendencies to just the little plastic lift-pegs that allow the back-seats to fold down.

I love the new car, since it can take me out to the *real* woods. It runs through mud like a mudpuppy (oops, Freudian spell slip! Apropos, don't you think?) and brandishes a "Life is Merrier with an Airedale Terrier" bumper sticker on the back. I miss the sunroof terribly, though.

McKinley

Dog's Name: **McKinley**
Breed: **Alaskan Husky**
Age: **Puppy**
Sex: **Female**
Owner: **Jodi Yann**
Location: **Portland, Oregon**
Damage: **$500**

I am an Alaskan Husky. When I was very small, my parents took me everywhere. It was great. Unfortunately, as I grew, they tended to leave me home more often.

I hate fences and leashes, but I love cars. I think I should be able to go wherever they do. So I started giving them hints. Every time they left me in the yard, I climbed over the fence or dug under it. They got the picture, and started taking me places.

Not long ago, they took me along when they went shopping. They thought I wouldn't mind waiting in the car. I did. I gave them five minutes; after that, I decided I was hungry, so I sampled the seat belts. They were tasty, plus they felt good to my new teeth. So I just occupied my time eating the seat belts until they came back.

I thought we were going to church next, because Mom kept saying, "Oh, my God. Oh, my God." But then she started crying and we went home.

I think she was upset, but I don't know what the big deal was. Those seat belts just grew right back in a week or so.

Zora

Dog's Name: **Zora**
Breed: **Golden Retriever**
Age: **3 years**
Sex: **Male**
Owner: **Victoria Coolbaugh**
Location: **Carson City, Nevada**
Damage: **$250**

I'm sure you can all understand that I love to go for rides in the car. It's my favorite thing, next to water and tennis balls!

One day, my dad had taken me to my grandpa's so I could run and play and chase rabbits. On our way home, I begged and whined and slobbered on Dad's head until he lowered the window for me. It was really cold, so Dad only put it down a few inches.

I managed to get my big ol' head out anyway, so I could smell all the yummy stuff out there. I was having a great time until this *big, huge* truck came whizzing by at, like, a hundred miles an hour.

I yanked my head in as fast as I could, so it would not get smacked by the truck, and *smash,* there went the window into a million little pieces.

It spooked my dad so bad that he almost drove off the road. We had to pull over because the wind was so strong and there were little pieces of glass flying everywhere.

Dad checked to make sure I was all right; I didn't have a scratch on me. The best part was I got to ride the rest of the way home in the front seat!

Patches

Dog's Name: **Patches**
Breed: **Australian Cattle Dog**
Age: **6 years**
Sex: **Female**
Owner: **Louanne Mooney**
Location: **Wisconsin**
Damage: **$500**

I really hate cars. Except to ride in, of course. But when they go flying down my road and I can't chase them because (I wonder why) I have to be kept in the yard, I get *really mad* and attack Mommy's car and try to beat it up.

Well, even I know that a car is just a little too big, even for a mighty Cattle Dog. So, I was going to have to take care of it a little bit at a time. Trying to find the weakest part of the little car, I zeroed in on the front bumper. I grabbed the rubbery part at the end and pulled. It took me a couple of weeks, but, sure enough, I finally had the whole corner pulled off.

Now, after that, I wasn't sure what the weakest spot would be, so I went for the tires. They were probably the softest spot. Time after time, I attacked that front tire—but nothing happened.

Then, one day, Mom was watching a football game (I think it was called the "Rose Bowl" and Wisconsin was playing). Anyway, it was a big deal and Daddy and she were yelling and stuff, so I decided I would go outside and try to beat up that car some more.

They made me wait until half-time and then Mommy went out with me— I couldn't wait to strut my stuff.

Pretty soon a car went down *my* road and I attacked that darn tire with everything I had. My hostility had been building for a long time. I bit into the side of the tire just as hard as I could. And then, "SSSSSSS" went the tire. "*I don't believe this!*" went Mommy.

Then, she went in and got Daddy to show her how proud she was of my new trick. Daddy said something about how the tire must have been bad to begin with—he just never gives me the credit I deserve.

Dad had to go out in the snow after the football game and put on another tire. Then, he moved the car down the driveway to the end "just in case" (whatever that means) and he had to get another tire for Mom the next day.

Mom says she wouldn't have believed that trick if she hadn't seen it herself. Since the first time, I have repeated that trick on four other tires with the same result—"SSSSSSS."

Now that I am 6 years old, though, I don't do the tire thing anymore. Mostly because I broke most of my teeth. I used to bite *really hard* into different tires I have flattened.

You know, for a long time after the third tire, Mommy parked that car way down at the bottom of the driveway. Then, she finally started parking at the top and *surprise* . . . I got her again.

Joe-Joe

Dog's Name: **Joe-Joe**
Breed: **Mix**
Age: **1 year**
Sex: **Male**
Owner: **Jeff**
Location: **Kentucky**
Damage: **$10**

Doggy toys are OK, but when you're teething, it's time to call in the big guns. That's what I did a while back, when I found the neighbor's yummy valve stems. I had chewed one up a few days earlier, but my *coup de grace* was the second tire, which I made go flat. I did such a good job on that tire that the neighbors left the minivan in the driveway all day so that I could work on the others.

Boy, was Jeff (my human) mad when the neighbors called to tell him that I'd chewed up their tires. He was better when he walked over to survey the damage and found that I'd chewed up the valve stem extenders, and the actual valve stems and tires were OK. I saw a look of relief wash over his face, because I was hiding in the shrubs nearby and doggy-chuckling the whole time.

Just to let everyone know I was not going to be outdone, I chewed up two gallons of the neighbors' windshield-washer fluid that same night, after everyone had gone to bed. Jeff had to make a special trip to buy automotive supplies that weekend! He got chrome extenders this time, just to give me more of a challenge . . .

CHAPTER 10
Off to the Vet

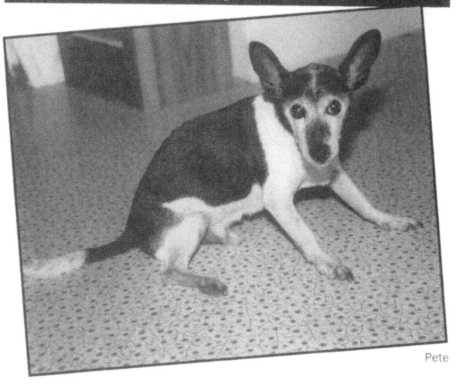

Pete

Dog's Name: **Pete**
Breed: **Mix**
Age: **11 years**
Sex: **Male**
Owners: **Ric and Darlene Dexter**
Location: **Cincinnati, Ohio**
Damage: **$1,000**

I really hate cats. Really hate 'em. One morning, when it was still dark, my mom let me out on the front porch. She usually looks outside first to make sure there are no cats, but this day she forgot.

When I got outside, there was a cat on *my* porch. He took off and I was right behind him! I would have got him, too, except I ran out of porch and jumped headlong into the darkness.

When I landed on the concrete driveway, I had traveled about 15 feet out and about 6 feet down. Well, after that, my left leg didn't work so well.

At the vet, there were a lot of "human sounds," but I remember only one sound—the tearing of an anterior cruciate ligament. I went to sleep and I didn't see Mom and Dad for two days!

Then they came and got me, but I had to stay in a cage for six weeks. I ate pretty well, though.

You know what? About a year later—just about the time the hair was growing back on my butt—I saw another cat in my yard! He ran right past me!

I started after him—my muscles rippling as I accelerated on the grass. All of a sudden my right leg didn't work so well—just sort of dragged behind me. Once again I heard those familiar "human sounds"—another torn anterior cruciate ligament.

Oh well, I ate pretty good . . .

Bailey

Dog's Name: **Bailey**
Breed: **Labrador Retriever**
Age: **3 years**
Sex: **Male**
Owner: **Brian Swalve**
Location: **The Woodlands, Texas**
Damage: **$1,700**

My masters decided that they wanted to have a break from me (black Lab) and my adopted sister Sandi (yellow Lab) last summer. So, they decided to take a three-week trip overseas.

They calculated that boarding us at a kennel all that time would easily cost them $400, not including playtime and air-conditioning (hey, it's hot in Texas in July!).

So they hatched a plan to leave Sandi and me at a friend's house ("summer camp," they told me) to save *beaucoup* bucks.

Desert me, would they? I'd show them. Only a day or two into their vacation, I devised my plan. I would run crazily around the yard at supersonic speeds until . . .

Oh my gosh . . . I ran into a sprinkler and tore my belly from between my front legs all the way back to my . . . well, you know where. Thank goodness my "camp parents" came home at lunch to check on me.

Off I went to the emergency room at the local vet clinic. They sewed me up and I spent the next three weeks with tubes hanging out of me. Of course, my intent to ruin my masters' vacation was spoiled because my "camp parents" were smart enough not to call them.

By the time they returned from vacation, I had racked up $1,700 worth of bills, and was given the vet center's "Trauma of the Month Award." That'll teach them to ever leave me alone for that length of time again.

Oh, by the way: I was only slowed down for about a month. I am back to running around full speed in my own yard, but you can be assured that my masters have removed any potentially sharp objects. Now I just run into large blunt objects and am dazed for a few seconds.

I want to say thanks to "camp parents" Jill and Chuck. They went way out of their way to take care of me. Also, thanks to the wonderful people at the Woodlands Pet Clinic. You did a great job.

Until my next adventure, run wild and fast.

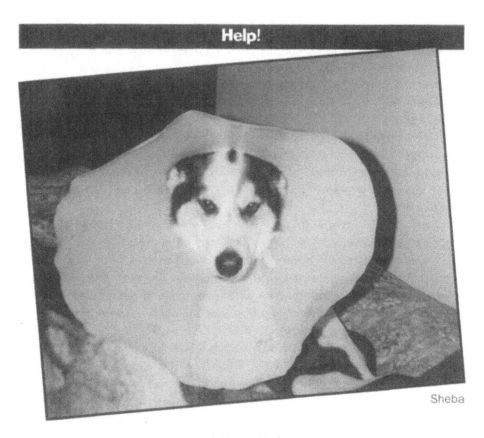

Sheba

Dog's Name: **Sheba**
Breed: **Malamute/Siberian Husky mix**
Age: **1 year**
Sex: **Female**
Owner: **Erika English**
Location: **Canada**
Damage: **$250**

I'm Sheba. Wolf and I have to stay in the basement every day until Mom comes back from work. We have to stay in this room that is especially made for us. We have lots of blankets, toys, bones and lots of branches to chew on.

At first, they put a 6-foot door on the opening, with sheets of metal screwed to it. The nerve!!!!! How are we supposed to bite through it!?! But I fooled them all. I jumped over it. First, I pooped all over the carpet. Then, I found a few things to chew on. I didn't want to overdo it, because I didn't want to get Mom too mad.

Then they made the door right up to the ceiling, but the one board was just half a foot too short and there was a space between the ceiling and wall about one half by one foot. The whole door was seven feet high. As if that could stop me! I half-jumped and half-climbed over it. What gave me away was the white fur I left behind on top of the door. Wolf is black.

Mom was amazed. She couldn't believe it. I'm a 70-pound Malamute/Siberian Husky. As far as she's concerned, I should not fit in such a tiny hole. Little does she know I am more fur than anything else. Poor Wolf just looked and whined because he couldn't get out.

In the process, I chewed some tools, any cardboard box I could find, blankets, a telephone and lots more.

Then they put a proper door on the opening, made out of two-by-fours and sheet metal. I was making progress. I had to reach really high and balance myself. Somehow I got caught on the metal and when I tried to pull away, I sliced my leg wide open to the bone. I didn't know what to do! I had to wait until Mom came home. It felt like hours and hours (maybe it was?). I just looked at Mom and she asked me why I looked at her with such sad eyes and then she bent down to give me a hug. Well, she took one look at my leg and within minutes we were in the car on the way to the vet.

They stitched me up. Mom waited three hours to take me back home. She was not going to leave me there overnight. I can't remember when she picked me up, because I was still almost asleep. But when I was really awake, guess what they did to me! They put something around my head. They called it a "cone."

I took it off the first day I was alone. Now they put my collar really tight and I have not been able to pull it over my head, but I learned that if I go sideways outside the dog door, I can actually get out!!! Coming in is a bit harder. The cone is bigger than the door, but it squishes together. That's my tale for now.

Jaco

Dog's Name: **Jaco**
Breed: **Labrador Retriever**
Age: **2 years**
Sex: **Male**
Owner: **Kari McCluskey**
Location: **Janesville, Wisconsin**
Damage: **$600**

My name is Jaco. I'm 108 pounds and I *love* balls of any kind. One day, my dad and I were playing with a golf ball in the field. He would toss it and I would bring it back. I was having a lot of fun until I *swallowed* the golf ball.

I didn't tell Dad. He thought we just lost it in the field. So we went home. A few days later, I found *another* golf ball in the field. I took it to my dad again and he tossed it. Whoops! I swallowed it again.

Dad looked around for it. I didn't say anything. By this time, I was starting to feel sick. I couldn't even eat. Mom took me to the vet. She thought I had the flu. I guess Dad must have said something about the balls because Mom said something to the vet.

The vet took an X ray and found two Titleist golf balls. I had to have an emergency operation. It was only $600. No big deal.

Mommy, Save Me From the Plastic Worm!

Dog's Name: **Watson**
Breed: **Portuguese Water Dog**
Age: **1 year**
Sex: **Male**
Owner: **Charlene Vickers**
Location: **Yellowknife, NWT, Canada**
Damage: **A Few Modifications to the Veterinarian's Office**

Last week, I peed on the carpet a few times without meaning to—I don't know why, it just came out—and Mom said I might have an infection or a stone. I like to play with stones, so this made me happy.

So we went to the evil veterinarian's. I say evil because you doggies won't believe what she did to me. The veterinarian waited until Mom was gone—so she couldn't rescue me—and then the vet took a white plastic worm and tried to *put it up my boyparts!* I screamed and howled, and the vet had to get her evil assistants to hold me down!

Later, Mom returned. I heard her and cried and howled "Help, Mom! Get this white worm out of my boyparts!" The evil assistant went and got me and was going to take the white worm out, but I escaped! I ran through the clinic, crashing into doors, bottles, jars, chairs, paperwork and anything I could find, going from room to room in a desperate attempt to find Mom so that she would know what they did to me. But the vet caught me first and took the worm out so Mom wouldn't see any evidence of my treatment.

I tried to tell her what had happened by barking all the details as loudly as possible right in her ear while standing on her chest (I had knocked her over by then). I then noticed all the other dogs with their people standing around staring at my mom as if she was a bad girl.

Of course, they all needed to be taught a lesson, so I went around making sure they knew who was the King—by humping them all. Mom was really mad, I think 'cause this stupid lady kept telling me, "Siiittt, dear," in a whiny voice, which I thought was funny. But I wouldn't sit because Mom is my master, not this lady.

Mom says I should win the award for the worst-behaved dog in a veterinary clinic in Canada this year. I think I was perfect—I can't help it if the evil vet and her evil assistants want to stick worms up my peeer!

Note from Watson's mom: Watson was catheterized and just about destroyed the entire clinic. I have never been so embarrassed in my life. Fortunately, he's not sick.

CHAPTER 11
Owners and Training

Rocky

Dog's Name: **Rocky**
Breed: **Golden Retriever**
Age: **Puppy**
Sex: **Male**
Owners: **Robert and Sue Sargent**
Location: **Buffalo, New York**
Damage: **A Few Toasted Brain Cells**

My owners, Bob and Sue, recently decided to install an invisible fence. For those who don't know, an invisible fence is a wire that's buried around the property and gives off a signal. When I have on a special collar and get near the wire, I first get a high-pitched noise. If I keep going I get a shock.

I watched carefully for two days as Bob buried the wire and hooked it all up to an electrical gizmo in the shed. The time had now come to test it out.

Tired, sweaty and anxious to try out the new system, Bob told Sue, "You go turn it on and I'll go get the collar and test it." With the special collar in his hand, he approached the buried wire to listen for the warning tone.

Now, I've told you he's stupid, but I also think he's going deaf because he couldn't hear the beeping as he got near the wire, so Bob yelled to Sue, "Turn up the power!" and she turned the dial on the gizmo way up. Still not hearing it, and thinking maybe it wasn't working, he put the collar up to his ear and went closer to the wire.

Then it happened . . . 6000 volts of electricity shot through Bob's head. As he stood there dazed, confused and standing straighter than I've ever seen him stand before, I turned to Sue and gave her that doggy-tilt-your-head look. She yelled out, "Is it working!?!"

Bob then mumbled something that no one could understand and went into the house for the manual. He returned much later, visibly shaken.

Now, for me the training went easy. I honestly don't even have to wear the special collar: The recollection of Bob's head lighting up like a Christmas tree is enough.

I still know where all the wire is buried, 'cause I watched him bury it. But, Bob's still not exactly sure, especially now that the grass has grown over it.

On occasions when we're in the yard and near the wire, I'll slowly walk over toward him till the collar beeps and watch his face twitch.

I'll take a look back at Sue, and I know we'll both be thinking, "What a jerk!"

Monty

Dog's Name: **Monty**
Breed: **Labrador Retriever**
Age: **1 year**
Sex: **Male**
Owners: **Steve Harvey and Leanne Copping**
Location: **Perth, Western Australia, Australia**
Damage: **$200**

I'm a lovable Labrador and my owners take me for walks most nights. Sometimes they stop for a coffee at our neighborhood cafe and I sit next to them and usually get fed a biscuit.

One night, they decided to try a different cafe that had just opened. When we arrived, they said I would have to wait outside because there were no outside tables. They tied me to a big potted plant with a tree in it and told me to sit while they went inside.

I tried sitting still, but next thing I knew, a dog went past in a car and barked at me, so I had to chase it. I was tied to the plant and when I took off, it fell over and the pot broke. Unfortunately, I still had the tree tied to my lead so when I ran down the street, the tree kept hitting me in the behind and I got very confused (who was that who kept hitting me?) and scared.

After my owners paid for the broken pot, new tree and two coffees, they said something about having just paid for the world's most expensive coffees ($100 each) and vowed never to take me out again.

Of course, I was able to charm them with my big brown eyes and I still go out with them most nights, but we never, ever stop at that cafe . . .

Sheba

Dog's Name: **Sheba**
Breed: **Mix**
Age: **7 years**
Sex: **Female**
Owner: **Karen Bannan**
Location: **Levittown, New York**
Damage: **$10**

om Karen and Dad Chris are so proud of me since I've gotten over my separation anxiety that they take me for lots of cool walks, especially Karen. Last Saturday, she wanted to go get the morning paper, so she and I walked about a mile to the corner deli in the local shopping center.

Mom tied me to a *huge, scary* can filled with garbage located right outside the shop and told me to wait and she'd bring me a treat. I waited about 10 seconds and decided that I wanted to follow her into the store.

I pulled at my leash and *bang!* All of a sudden, the can flipped onto its side and started following me! I was scared, so I started running!

Mom Karen came out of the shop and started calling to me, but by that time, it was too late. The can was chasing me and I was running as fast as I could to get away. I had my tail tucked under my body and I kept scrunching my butt as close to my head as I could.

Since it was early on a beautiful, warm Saturday, everyone came running out of the other shops in the center and started pointing and *laughing!*

Meanwhile, the can continued to chase me and throw its litter cargo everywhere. Mom Karen was laughing, too! That meanie! She kept screaming, "Stop Sheba! Stop!"

The can finally caught me and stopped me on a curb, more than 50 feet from my original starting place. Mom Karen came over and untied me from the can and retied me to a sturdy tree.

Then she spent 15 minutes picking up garbage and dragging the can all over the parking lot. The whole time she was muttering, "Stupid dog. How embarrassing. Everyone is looking at me and knows what a silly dog I own."

Meanwhile, every human in the parking lot kept coming up and laughing at me, asking Karen if I did that often. Duh—as if I like running from cans and Karen likes cleaning garbage!

When Karen was done cleaning up the parking lot (personally, I think she picked up a lot more garbage than was originally in the can), she stopped in the shade next to me and called Dad on the cellular phone. She told him the whole story!

Karen started laughing hysterically again and I could even hear Dad laughing, too. The worst part was, they called all their friends and relatives and told *them* about my escape from the angry garbage can. Bah! How rude!

Now, when we go for a walk, Karen ties me to a tree or a pole that's stuck into the ground and she never leaves me for more than one minute without checking on me or asking someone to keep an eye on me. All I can say is, how humiliating!

Schatzi

Dog's Name: **Schatzi**
Breed: **Weimaraner**
Age: **Puppy**
Sex: **Female**
Owner: **Lisa Brown**
Damage: **A Soot-Covered Mom**

It all started one cold, rainy night. We all loved to get a fire going in the fireplace, share a bowl of popcorn and listen to the rain pattering down outside. Well, I went out with Mom to get some wood for the fire, and we hauled in a lot of logs. I helped a lot by standing on the patio cheering her on with my best barking voice, for I certainly wasn't going to go out and get *my* feet cold and wet!

After Mom got the fire going, popped the corn and sat down all comfy, I stood in front of her playing the "catch-a-falling-popcorn" game. I was really good at this game, and Mom didn't notice, but my telepathic eyes caused her to give me the biggest share of the whole bowl!

We were just feeling full and I curled up for a nice snooze in front of the fire when, *whizzz*, something passed by my head.

I noticed that Mom looked my way, with that "What are you doing now?" look. I, of course, just adjusted my halo.

Well, *whizzz*, and *whizzz*, and *whizzz* and soon I was up and *so* happy that Mom had planned this surprise for me! Carpenter bees were coming out of the log in the fireplace! Even better, they were groggy from the heat and smoke, so they were just flopping around the room. I barked and barked, and jumped over furniture to show Mom how much I loved this neat surprise she had for me.

Mom didn't seem very happy about my joy—she was yelling, "No, no, you'll get stung! Leave it! Leave it!" I jumped over the coffee table, hot on the wings of one of these whizzers, spilling Mom's coffee all over some papers she was going to correct for her fourth-grade students.

She ran from the room yelling, "Schatzi, come!" Of course, I always did what Mom asked and I went with her. She shut me into another room; I imagine she was keeping all the fun by the fire for herself. I had never known her to be at all selfish before!

Anyway, she was armed with a flyswatter and a broom, and all kinds of other things—and then she opened the door to the outside and carried that burning log out into the rain and dumped it in a big puddle. Of course, the room got cold, Mom was covered with soot and all the fun whizzers were gone.

I really thought that Mom looked pretty funny, but I decided it wasn't a good time to jump on her and let her know it. I was kind of sorry that she stopped the fun game with the Whizzers so soon. I could have gone on playing for a lot longer.

CHAPTER 12
Trouble with the Law

Danny Boy

Dog's Name: **Danny Boy**
Breed: **English Cocker Spaniel**
Age: **6 years**
Sex: **Male**
Owners: **Jim and Judy**
Damage: **False Alarm**

Like some other fun-loving troublemakers, I've been responsible for getting the cops to our house. Maybe the sheriff's department should write a book about "Dog Calls."

Anyhow, my Sheriff Department Dog Call began when Mom came home alone one night from a meeting. Mom had been gone all day at work, and then away to this stupid meeting. Anything that keeps her away from me, Candy and Cookie is stupid.

So, when Mom came home, I was awfully excited. You see, I love her the most. This time, I jumped up on the front door just as she was trying to open it. The door slammed in her face. I was only jumping up to greet her, but my timing was off a little. (Just a tiny mistake on my part.)

There had been a few robberies in the neighborhood and Mom didn't know it was me who slammed the door, so she wasn't going to enter the house alone after that. She thought there might be a robber inside. Like, who's going to come in here with three Cocker Spaniels ready to do battle!?! Those other houses did not have fine guard dogs like us on duty.

Anyway, because Mom had not gone in to punch up the security code, the burglar alarm went off and was wailing like there's no tomorrow.

You've never heard such racket as when the cops arrived. House alarm going off. Helicopter flying overhead with spotlight glaring. Police invading our house with flashlights and guns. It was very scary, actually. Well, I mean, Candy and Cookie were scared. I am a dude, so of course I wasn't bothered by all the fuss. (Well, fireworks make me cry. But let's not talk about that.)

It was nice to have such distinguished company in the house. The police were very thorough. They found Candy and Cookie hiding. I tried to get the cops to throw me a tennis ball, but they didn't take the hint.

It was very considerate of the deputies not to laugh in front of Mom. I think they must have waited until they got back to the sheriff substation. My mom is a former mayor of our city, so she was embarrassed by the incident.

But, I didn't slam the door on purpose. It wasn't really my fault. If Mom wouldn't go away to stupid work or meetings, I wouldn't need to miss her so much and jump up and down when I know she's finally home. As I said earlier, I love her the most.

Talon

Dog's Name: **Talon**
Breed: **German Shepherd**
Age: **1 year**
Sex: **Male**
Owner: **Robert J. Lessels**
Location: **Madison, Alabama**
Damage: **A Wet Kitty**

My first mom couldn't feed all of us. She had a wolf, a lion cub and seven cats! That darned lion cub she was raising for a game farm ate enough for all eight of us—so she gave me away.

My new dad has a nice home with a six-foot-high fence, which he thinks I can't get over. Not that I have to—he's really good about taking me for walks whenever he can.

He sensed I was lonely—some humans are good at sensing a dog's feelings, y'know—so he got me a pet of my own. I think I'd rather have had a German Shepherdess, but then I'm neutered so . . . Anyway, what I got was a kitten.

When my dad and I would go for our really long walks, my kitten would try to tag along. Being a kitten, though, she wasn't up to the three-mile jaunts Dad and I took each day. About a half mile from home, she'd sit down and make these funny noises—"mew, mew." Sniffing her didn't stop them, nor did giving her a big old wet slobbery lick. So I finally just picked her up by the scruff of her neck just like I'd seen Momma cat do at my first home.

She stopped making those funny noises and just swung there from my jaws, watching the world go by, as Dad and I walked along. Anyway, Dad, the kitten and I were strolling along when people started yelling and pointing at us. Dad smiled and waved back but they were still making loud noises. When we got home, Dad hit the shower and the kitten started washing herself—baths, yuck! Then there was this pounding on the door. I stood up on the doorframe and looked down out of the top panel of glass to see this guy in a uniform from the local animal control office. He looked up at me and got this really sick look on his face. You'd think he'd never seen a seven-foot-long, 140-pound German Shepherd.

By this time, Dad's out of the shower and telling me to go lay down. I plopped in my favorite corner and the kitten—kind of damp from her own bath—jumped up and snuggled into my fur to sleep.

The guy in the uniform saw this and started laughing. He told my dad that the neighbors had called him thinking I'd caught my kitten and was gonna eat her.

What am I, a cannibal? She's family! Sheeeesh! The guy in the uniform called the neighbors and Dad let everyone see that the kitten was OK. Everyone started laughing—well, everyone but the kitten—she just started snoring.

Now that she's all grown up, the cat doesn't need my help anymore. She runs alongside with us now, darting from bush to bush and making sure we're not ambushed by any mice. Dad calls us his John Steinbeck Personal Security System—one for mice, one for men.

Now, if I could just convince the rest of the neighborhood cats that I'm really friendly when I run over to greet them . . .

My $100 Patch

Dog's Name: **Sheena**
Breed: **Australian Cattle Dog**
Age: **7 years**
Sex: **Female**
Owner: **David Wunderlich**
Location: **Phoenix, Arizona**
Damage: **$100**

My owner, Dave, took me on a trip to Tucson. I love going to Tucson. There's lots to see, sniff and do, and lots 'n' lots of wide open areas to run around in.

I love the outdoors and I love to herd things. It doesn't matter what it is—cows, sheep or children. I tried butterflies once, but that didn't work. If it moves, I'll herd it. I even herded peacocks once—and got Dave in a lot of trouble, too.

Peacocks in Arizona? *Yup!* Dave used to take me to this huge park that was once one of the largest citrus groves in the Phoenix area. Now it is a historical monument with three houses; a canal (one of the first canals bringing water into Phoenix); lots of citrus trees; and several baseball, soccer and volleyball fields.

It also has a beautiful rose garden, fountains, slides and swings and, as I mentioned before, peacocks. I don't know why they have peacocks at the park. Dave says that he heard a park ranger talking about how the original owners used to breed them for their feathers. I guess women back in the 1890s liked their feathers for hats, clothes and dusters.

All I know is that they are everywhere and, being an Australian Cattle Dog, I like order. It seemed to me that they should all be in one place.

Now, Dave didn't let me off of my leash often, but there came a point in my training (I was training to be a desert search-and-rescue dog at the time) that it was necessary for me to be off my leash for extended periods of time.

You will probably not believe me, but I waited a whole 10 minutes (I have some self-control) before I headed out at breakneck speed to round up all of those birds. Barking and nipping, I chased all of them around the houses, out of the citrus groves and into a corner of one of the main fields.

It wasn't long before I had finished my job that a park ranger came running out to greet Dave and me to congratulate us on a job well done. After all, I had created order from chaos.

Much to my surprise, the ranger started screaming at Dave while waving his arms in the air and occasionally pointing at me. I was starting to get a little bit concerned that the ranger was going to hurt Dave, so I started barking and baring my teeth—just a little bit, though. Just wanted to show him that I wasn't going to let him hurt Dave.

He calmed down real quick, and Dave put me back on the leash. The ranger scribbled on a piece of paper, handed the piece of paper to Dave and then called a couple of other rangers on his two-way radio.

Dave was not happy about whatever the ranger wrote (turned out it was a $100 fine), but the rangers were happy after they had counted the peacocks and announced that all 47 birds were accounted for.

As it turns out, they have to count all of the peacocks at the end of the month and I had made it much easier for them to do so. They were grateful.

In fact, this was the first time in four months that they had gotten an accurate count, so they gave me a park ranger patch. Dave refers to it as my $100 patch.

Since then, Dave has never let me off the leash at that park and we've found another field for my training. I still like to herd things, although the opportunities to do so are not what they once were.

Dog's Name: **Brutus (aka Rex)**
Breed: **Great Pyrenees/St. Bernard mix**
Age: **4 years**
Sex: **Male**
Owner: **Laurie Sheriff**
Location: **Oregon**
Damage: **Trapped Officer**

I'm such a big, beautiful dog that people stop and point at me while my human takes me on walks. According to that evil veterinarian human, I'm one of the biggest dogs he has ever seen.

Late one summer night, my human came home from an evening of champagne and revelry at a wedding reception. She dutifully put me on my leash and we went out for a late-night stroll. It was quite pleasant roaming the quiet streets so *very* late at night.

Imagine my human's surprise when we came home and she realized she had locked us out of the house. Resourceful human that she is, she waved down a passing police officer and used her considerable charm to coax him into breaking into our house for us. He wiggled his way into a window, and grandly opened the door for us to enter.

Meanwhile, I was dozing in the cool grass, and awoke to find a strange man peering out of *my* front door. I leapt to the aid of my human, certain I was protecting her from a nefarious scoundrel.

I jerked the leash out of her hand and ran snarling to the man in blue. He slammed the door shut, and roamed from window to window, peering fearfully out to check on my whereabouts. My human trailed after me, foolishly yelling "Sit! Stay!" as I circled the house, snarling and barking.

After much yelling on the part of both humans, and barking by me, the police officer scampered from the house and into his car and made a break for somewhere safe.

My human still giggles over the night I saved her from the police officer inside *our* house!

CHAPTER 13

Jealousy and Embarrassment

Max, left; Madison, right

Dog's Name: **Max**
Breed: **Chihuahua**
Age: **3 years**
Sex: **Male**
Owners: **John and Traci Bruce**
Location: **Florida**
Damage: **$10**

I'm Max, the smartest, sweetest, cutest Chihuahua in the world. You'd think that having me would be enough, but Mom and Dad got me a sister, Madison, a Cocker Spaniel. She's too embarrassed to tell this story, so I will.

When Mom has to go in to work at night or on weekends when nobody else is there, she lets us come, too. We get to run around and check everybody's trash cans for leftover food.

When Mom takes breaks, she'll run with us and play hide-and-seek. We never understand why we can't go every day with her, or why she complains sometimes about going. We always have fun there.

We were there one night and I'd raided all the trash cans and had come back to settle in Mom's lap while she worked. Madison was still exploring. She was under and almost behind a desk when she stepped on something that stuck to her foot. She got out from under the desk and tried to walk away from the sticky thing, but it stayed with her.

She sat down to try to get it off her foot and the rest of it stuck to her butt and the back of her legs. Then she tried to run away from it, but it was stuck! So she got scared and started screaming. Mom nearly dumped me on the floor, she jumped up so fast!

When Mom found her, she started laughing! Madison had gotten her butt stuck to one of those glue strips they use to catch mice. Mom had to pull it off of her, which looked like it hurt.

Then, we had to go home, even though Mom wasn't done working yet. On the way home, Madison got stuck to a plastic bag that was in the backseat. She had to get a bath and our neighbor had to come over and help hold her down so Mom could cut all the glue off Madison's butt, legs and feet.

The next morning, Mom had to tell the guy who put out the glue strips what happened so he didn't think that there was a huge black rat that escaped from the glue strip and was running around the office. The whole glue strip was covered with black hair and was in a different room!

I'm way too intelligent for anything like that to happen to me, but my sister . . . Well, Mom still calls her "Glue Butt" sometimes.

Max

Dog's Name: **Max**
Breed: **Lab/Terrier mix**
Age: **7 years**
Sex: **Male**
Owner: **David Simek**
Location: **Babylon, New York**
Damage: **A Sore Leg**

love to unwrap presents and shred the wrapping paper all over the house. I'm especially good at finding the packages with chocolate candies in them, even when they're on the top of the refrigerator!

Anyway, my human sister had a birthday party (3 years old—big deal!). I was having a blast helping her rip into the packages. But she was *soooo* slow, I started to get ahead of her.

About this time, her parents dragged me out of the house and into the backyard. I barked and barked, but nobody would pay attention to me. I only wanted to be part of the fun!

So, I made a running leap and jumped the 5-foot picket fence and ran to the front door to watch the party. They let me back in, but then dragged me right back to the backyard again.

I thought, "This calls for a real pathetic act." So, I ran to leap the fence, and when I got on the top, I wedged my back leg between the pickets, which caused me to hang from the fence. I then let out a blood-curdling scream.

The party stopped dead in its tracks—everybody came running outside to *me!!!* Human Dad gently lifted me off the fence and carried me into the house.

I became the center of attention and I stayed in the house for the rest of this party and every party since.

Caution: Pups, this is a dangerous trick—use it only as a last resort—but it is highly effective.

My Pirate

Dog's Name: **My Pirate**
Breed: **Chihuahua**
Age: **1 year**
Sex: **Female**
Owner: **Laura C. Patterson**
Location: **Metairie, Louisiana**
Damage: **Loss of Future Invitations**

My owner (well, actually, *I* own *her,* but that's another story) was having a shower for her daughter and there were a lot of nice ladies there. They all petted and snuggled my tiny body and I *love* that!

There was one lady who put me down every time I ran up her chest to kiss her face—the *nerve!* I left the room, then came back to this unsociable lady and, standing at a respectful distance, gently tapped her hand with my paw.

I finally got her attention and she said, "Oh look, she's got something in her mouth—she's brought me a present!" She put her hand out and I dropped a big piece of poop in it and pranced away!

Ignore me? Never!

Hershey

Dog's Name: **Hershey**
Breed: **Chesapeake Bay Retriever**
Age: **1 year**
Sex: **Male**
Owners: **Mark and Sherry Akins**
Location: **Watauga, Texas**
Damage: **Soiled Clothing**

I love to jump on the fence in my big backyard. Kids are always running up and down the sidewalk, and I may be a big dog, but I'm a puppy at heart—I just want to play!

Well, one day, I was really bad and stuck my head out too far. Mom got mad! To teach me a lesson, she decided to nail a board on the bottom of the fence to keep me in. I just couldn't stand it.

I got into big trouble when I decided to take my frustration out on her. I couldn't nudge her away and she kept pounding. So I walked up behind her and relieved myself on her back.

Not a good idea!

Dog's Name: **Cody**
Breed: **Rottweiler**
Age: **1 year**
Sex: **Male**
Owner: **Unknown**
Location: **Central California**
Damage: **$25**

My name's Cody, also known as Codeman. I really don't think this story belongs here, but for some reason my people do.

I love my family very much. In fact, my man found me thin and starving, abandoned on a back hills road during the winter. He was riding his motorcycle and tucked me into his motorcycle's saddlebag for the ride home. Great home and family—I really can't complain.

I live in a wonderful home on several acres of land in the hills. Remember, I said I was intelligent. Well, I usually have the better part of the day to fill with my own mischief. I love to go visit the neighbor's pool. I only spend an hour or so there, then I shake, dry out in the sun and head out to my next adventure. The neighbors don't even mind anymore.

Well, the story I'm about to tell occurred at Christmas time. I noticed that another neighbor, who I don't usually visit, had done something very strange to his house. He put up lights. All different colors and they came on and went off. Very strange, so I nosed on over for a closer look.

It wasn't as interesting as I thought it would be, so my investigation was quick. As I was getting ready to leave and find my couple, I realized that nature was calling. So, in lieu of a hydrant or tree, I hiked my leg and let go, right on the string of lights. (*Wowsers!!*) Out went the lights.

Now, this had become more than interesting. In fact, it was a bit painful, even shocking. I let out a blood-curdling howl and ran for home. I even beat my couple home.

It took a few hours of licking and shaking before I felt better. I sure got a lot of attention, and the family got a whole lot of laughter at my expense.

Needless to say, I stay away from that house from now on. I prefer pools to pretty tinkling lights.

Wedding Bell Blues

Dog's Name: **Brandy**
Breed: **Cairn Terrier**
Age: **2 years**
Sex: **Female**
Owners: **Debby and Chris Owen**
Location: **Tucker, Georgia**
Damage: **$50**

My humans and I went to another town for a wedding. The humans had the nerve to leave me alone in a bedroom with their wedding day finery (both were in the wedding party, not getting married that day). I knew this could not go unpunished.

I also knew that this had to be the male human's fault. His tuxedo lay below the female human's gown. I leaped on the bed, gently peeled back the dress to leave the tux exposed. I then proceeded to urinate on the tux.

My humans (once they got over their tantrum) spoke many times to other humans of this punishment. It's so nice to have well-trained humans!

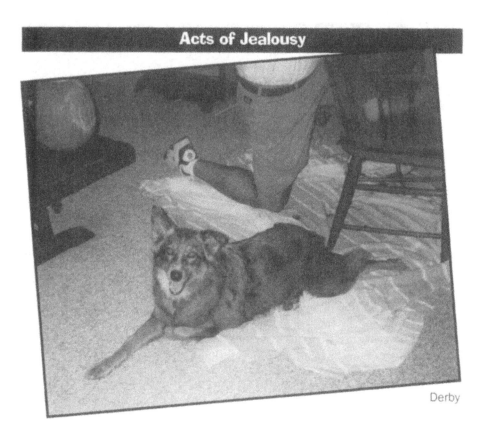

Derby

Dog's Name: **Derby**
Breed: **Australian Shepherd**
Age: **6 years**
Sex: **Female**
Owner: **Anonymous**
Location: **Florida**
Damage: **Embarrassment**

I'll admit it. I was jealous. My mom-human had just found a new friend. I can't really say that I didn't like him, because he has always been quite nice to me, at least for someone who dreads the touch of dog hair. But, he was just around too much, and I didn't like sharing my mom-human with him. I'll admit that it had a bad effect on my attitude. I did things that I really never would have done otherwise . . .

Like the night that I locked both of them out of the house. I had locked my human out many times, by accident, when I would paw the door to get out where she was. My paw would land right at the deadbolt and flip it into the locked position.

But, this time, I'll admit, was no accident. That was bad, I know, but what made it worse was that they didn't have any clothes on when I locked them out!!!! They were very upset with me, and if it hadn't been for the piece of wire off the grill that they used to unlock the door, I'm sure they would have been even madder.

Risk

Dog's Name: **Risk**
Breed: **Mix**
Age: **2 years**
Sex: **Male**
Owner: **Kymberly Foster-Seabolt**
Location: **Alliance, Ohio**
Damage: **Soggy Tools**

I am a very happy-go-lucky, inquisitive dog. On a sunny summer afternoon, I was valiantly attempting to help my dad, Mike, and a couple of his pals do a little construction work on the back of the house (he needs my help on these things, you know).

So there I was being a good little apprentice and helping him by sitting on his tools so they wouldn't run away and sniffing all the two-by-fours to make sure they were good before he used 'em, and what does he do? He yells at me!

I couldn't believe it. I was shocked, I tell you, just shocked! Mom keeps telling Dad that I am a very sensitive guy and that he shouldn't yell at me.

This time, I was really mad because not only did he yell at me, but then the big ol' baby stomped off into the house to get another screwdriver. If the big grump had just asked me, I could've told him that it was right under the truck where I'd put it so it would be safe.

So Mr. Grouch goes wailing off into the house and then tells Mom how "stupid" I am. Well! A guy can take just so much, and when he yells at me in front of outsiders and tells Mom those awful lies—that was just the last straw!

I glanced around to be sure he wasn't looking, circled a few times to get the feel of my plan and then lifted my leg and peed with perfect accuracy right into his toolbox. Now he knew right where his silly old tools were. Floating in his toolbox. Served him right, too!

It actually worked out well. Mom told him she thought it was the perfect response to his rudeness and his friends said my response was far from "stupid." I seemed pretty darn smart to them.

Bill

Dog's Name: **Bill**
Breed: **Mix**
Age: **4 years**
Sex: **Male**
Owners: **Bonnie Guess and Jerry Morris**
Location: **Florida**
Damage: **One Reputation**

I'm just an old bull kind of dog. Bill the Dog. That's me.

My story is about my most embarrassing moment. I'm 11 years old now, but the story you're about to hear happened when I was a mere lad and a "bit too cocky for my collar." All you bad dogs out there know what I mean.

Anyway, I was 4 years old when Mom, Dad and me went to St. Augustine by boat for the weekend. We had spent the night on the boat, and were docked at a marina the next morning. My mom was still snoozing down in the cabin on the boat. I got up with my dad (you know how us boys gotta stick together).

Well, I had to you-know-what really, really, really, bad. My dad noticed this right off the bat (being the clever fellow that he is) 'cause I was jumping around like I had ants in my pants.

Now, I don't mean to brag or anything, but being the highly trained, well-disciplined "Dude" that I am, I always, I repeat, always (yea, right!) wait for permission before getting off the boat.

So, I'm standing there waiting for my dad to give the "Okey-Dokey" to get off the boat, when he finally says, "Okay, Bill."

Yippee!!!!! Here I go!!! I get a running start and sail over the side of the boat—right smack dab in the water!!!!! Yikes!!!

In all my haste, "Dummy" me jumped off the wrong side of the boat!!! I was so embarrassed, I could have just sunk to the bottom right then and there.

Dad's laughing at me, all the people on the other boats are laughing at me and here I am, paddling around in the water like a fish.

Well, my mom, clad only in her underwear and T-shirt, heard the splash and came running from the cabin! This brings another roar of laughter from the gathering crowd of onlookers.

Now, I still don't know how Mama did it, 'cause, at 72 pounds, I'm pretty much an "oinker," but she grabbed me by the collar and lifted me up into the boat.

By this time, she was crying, I was crying and the crowd (which had grown even larger) was laughing so hard that they were crying!!!

After my mama dried me off and hugged and kissed me (I liked that part, she's such a sucker), I was okay physically, but I'm still in therapy . . .

Tanna, left; Moffit, center; Max, right

Dogs' Names: **Max, Tanna, Moffit**
Breed: **Schipperkes**
Ages: **4, 3 and 2 years**
Sexes: **Two Females and a Male**
Owner: **Dr. Mitzi Scotten**
Location: **Kansas City, Missouri**
Damage: **Social Disgrace**

I'm Max, the eldest of a clan of three Schipperkes. As surrogate children, we have had to endure numerous, sometimes degrading, instances in which our owner has put various forms of apparel on us and expected that we would be unfazed.

You would think, after two years, she would have figured out that Schipperkes do not wear clothing! There are those mellow mutts out there who will sacrifice their pride by wearing raincoats and galoshes—but not us!

I'm hoping that our latest outing has finally shown our doting mother that on the issue of clothes, and that includes costumes of any type, we will continue our zero-tolerance policy.

Last week, we were transported to a large pet store for what we thought was a well-deserved outing. Our owner had been tempted by a local Halloween costume contest for pets by the lure of first prize—a year's worth of free dog food.

To our horror, we found that once inside the store, we were suddenly submitted to a degrading spectacle, which included putting us each in a confining and somewhat scary Halloween outfit. Obviously, none of the three of us cared whether we kept in costume or character.

For the humans, we were to be the characters from the Wizard of Oz: the Tin Man, the Lion and the Scarecrow. Our mother was dressed as Dorothy. In fact, when it was our turn to walk in front of the crowd, I was the only one still in full costume. Tanna and Moffit were too busy shredding each other's costumes and then trying to pick fights with other contestants. Moffit ended the whole ordeal by lifting his leg in front of the judges and blessing the crowd with an extra-long urinary shower.

I am hoping that after this last show of solidarity, we will never again appear in public in bandanas, hats or any other attire, but I've already heard talk of next year, and something about "sedation" before the event! Oh well!

Madison

Dog's Name: **Madison**
Breed: **Cocker Spaniel**
Age: **Puppy**
Sex: **Female**
Owners: **John and Traci Bruce**
Location: **Florida**
Damage: **Embarrassment**

Failing in my attempts to be bad, I changed tactics. Now, I'm working on embarrassing my mom and dad as much as possible.

The other night, Mom and I were playing with my squeaky ball. I went out on the porch to take a break and cool off by lying on the concrete. Of course, I took my squeaky ball with me. I like looking through the bars on our balcony, and I accidentally dropped my squeaky ball into the bushes below. Mom saw me do it and sent Dad to go get it. Aren't they great?

I figured this might be a new game, so later I dropped it off again. Mom said forget it, she wasn't going to get my ball for me all night. So, a few hours later, it was time to go to bed and Mom decided she would go get my ball before lights out.

Since it was dark, the ball was really hard to see and she wasn't exactly sure where I dropped it. I guess she was making a lot of noise beating the bushes for my ball, because she woke up our new downstairs neighbor.

The neighbor turned on all of her outside lights and peeked through the blinds. There was Mom, playing in the bushes right outside the new neighbor's glass door at 11:30 at night.

Mom got really embarrassed and came back upstairs. The neighbor watched her the whole way. She got my ball the next morning and had to apologize for scaring the neighbor and explain why she was playing in the bushes that late at night. It was really funny!

They've got me in obedience class now, too. I really don't know what's going on.

Wash His Mouth Out with Soap

Dog's Name: **Dusty**
Breed: **Doberman Pinscher**
Age: **2 years**
Sex: **Male**
Owner: **Michael Quinn**
Location: **Maryland**
Damage: **No Church This Sunday**

It was a hot summer day, so I decided to take a break from chasing cats and take a little nap under the front porch. My owner was in the house washing dishes and trying to listen to *The Young and the Restless* on the TV.

All of a sudden, the front door of the house flew open and a large man ran into the room shouting four-letter words, screaming like a maniac. My owner took a pot she was washing and, yelling and screaming, threw it at the man. I was close on his heels, and within seconds had him on the floor in the living room.

Finally, the man gained a little sanity and explained he was a minister of a local church and was going door to door inviting people to join his church. He had already knocked on the door when I awoke from my nap and came out from under the porch to stretch.

When he saw me yawn, he thought I was going to bite him so he panicked. Needless to say, he was more than a little embarrassed about bursting in the door and the language he used.

I don't think he is doing much door-to-door in my neighborhood. At least he'll know to look under porches and to let sleeping dogs lie.

CHAPTER 14
Oops!

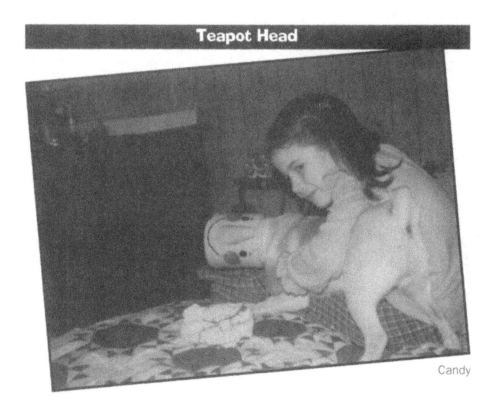

Candy

Dog's Name: **Candy**
Breed: **Pug**
Age: **Puppy**
Sex: **Female**
Owner: **Anne G. Musser**
Location: **New Jersey**
Damage: **One Teapot**

I'm just a new puppy. My mom puts me in the bathroom when she goes to work so that I don't annoy my big brother.

She makes sure the shower curtain is tucked in so I don't eat a chunk and choke. She makes sure the lid is down so I don't go for a swim and drown. But the teapot she used to water plants and wash the tub never crossed her mind. But, being a curious pup, it certainly crossed mine.

One day, that bright blue teapot was just too enticing. I got it off of the edge of the tub and started playing with it. The next thing I knew, my head was stuck inside. Now how could that have happened?

Boy, was my mommy surprised when she came home and found my cute little puppy body topped with a blue teapot where my head should be!

Mommy pulled and pulled, but the teapot wouldn't come off. She took a knife and sawed the end off of the teapot so that I could breathe and get a drink of water. Lucky for me that I have a pug nose!

She pulled and pulled some more. Nope, looked like it was stuck. She finally had to take me to a neighbor who was on the rescue squad. He cut that mean old teapot off of my head with some tin snips. It was a terrible experience, but not terrible enough to keep me out of future catastrophes.

I intend to remain a curious pup.

Moskey

Dog's Name: **Moskey**
Breed: **Dachshund**
Age: **2 years**
Sex: **Male**
Owners: **Benjamin Klein and Ann Yehle**
Location: **Madison, Wisconsin**
Damage: **Tummy Left Wanting**

So there I was, sitting in Mom and Dad's Jeep. We were driving along and I started to sniff the bags in the trunk. Hmmm . . . I'd know that smell anywhere . . . *Steak!!!*

Of course the steak was for me, so I started to crawl in there to get it. Suddenly, Dad turned around and yelled, "Moskey, *no!* blah blah blah!" "Oh ho, what's this? Some steak sitting there, taunting my nose, and it's not for me? We'll see about that."

Anyhow, I bide my time. If there's anything that comes naturally to a fine Dachshund like myself, it's persistence, but I've come to realize that if I pretend I've given up, the best opportunities seem to come my way.

Sure enough, we stopped the Jeep again. Mom and Dad talked for awhile, I don't know, something about a "video." Mom got out of the Jeep and went into some store. I was a little upset at first, but Dad's a good guy and he wouldn't let her go in alone if she needed protection. Still, I barked a little, just to be safe. Dad and I were left eyeing each other.

That darn Dad knows all my tricks; he could see the little gears working in my head about the steak. I knew better than to make my move then. Then, all of a sudden, Dad got this great idea. A little light bulb went on above his head. He said to me "Mossy, I've got a great idea for a video that Mom can rent. Can you be good for a minute while I run in and tell her?"

Of course, I played it cool. I was thinking, "Sure I'll be good—sucker!" Dad knew this, but he was really sweating because he didn't want to end up watching *Lethal Weapon 2* again.

Suddenly, he made a break for it. I saw him sprinting into the store, but he wasn't the only one hustling. I dove into the back and started working on the steak package. Tick . . . Tick . . . Tick . . . Man, that plastic just wouldn't go . . . *Finally!*

I lifted my head in triumph, my prize clamped between my jaws. "Oh! Uh . . . Hi Dad! Uh . . . Is this your steak?" My jaws open in chagrin, the hard-won steak drops.

Next time, I'll just *eat* the darn package . . .

Mouth Wide Shut

Dog's Name: **Rex**
Breed: **Jack Russell Terrier**
Age: **1 year**
Sex: **Male**
Owner: **Mary Milloway**
Location: **Pennsylvania**
Damage: **Recurring Nightmares**

I love my lady; she's so wonderful. To tell you the truth, I'm a little obsessed with her. She tells me that if I were a human I would be her stalker. I do like to be with her almost all the time.

I say *almost* all the time, because sometimes I feel the need to do things that she just wouldn't like. You know, like chase the dumb cats or chew up a pool cue or eat stuff I shouldn't. The last one got me in some trouble. The eating stuff I shouldn't.

I didn't know that I shouldn't eat it. After all, my girl Mallory gave it to me. But then, Mallory gave the fish a drink of Kool-Aid because they looked thirsty—maybe that should have warned me.

Anyway, Mallory gave me some brown taffy. At first, it was very nice—sweet and chewy. Yum. But, then I couldn't stop chewing. I chewed and chewed, then I couldn't chew anymore. I couldn't get my jaws apart. The taffy stuck my mouth shut.

I started to get scared and ran to my lady. I kept following her around and *looking* at her, you know, trying to get her attention. But she just thought I was being an emotional sponge trying to gain affection. She didn't realize how serious this was; I couldn't bark or eat or chew. Life as I know it ceased.

Well, I really started to get panicked; I started to cry and drool. My lady then looked at me and realized something was wrong. She picked all that taffy out from between my teeth. I loved her for that.

Best of all, I didn't get in trouble for eating the taffy—Mallory got into trouble for giving it to me!

Jump!

Dog's Name: **Tristan**
Breed: **Mix**
Age: **11 years**
Sex: **Male**
Owner: **Mary Milloway**
Location: **Pennsylvania**
Damage: **$50**

I love my humans, and, frankly, I get a little anxious when they leave. Usually, I'll just grab the odd bit of food off the counter. You know, like a loaf of bread, some cookies. Or, if worst comes to worst, some cat food will have to do. I need to have something to nosh on, or at least lick.

One time, my humans said they were going on vacation, and Uncle K. would be in to see me, feed me, etc. I like Uncle K. He's a dog guy. I was OK, and the anxiety level was manageable. We said our good-byes.

Then, I was left alone.

The anxiety mounted. I have to admit, I ate everything in sight, except the cats. There was no relief to the anxiety . . . The tension mounted . . . I chewed a couple of window frames, to no avail. Then, I remembered the bathroom. There was a screen in the window . . . a way out . . . I had to get out!

I ran up the steps, pushed the screen window out and was on the back porch roof. I was OK for awhile, until I realized that I couldn't get down, or back inside.

To top it off, all those darn cats came out with me. "Jump, Tristan, jump," they said, "It's only 12 feet." They snickered. I looked down and decided jumping wasn't an option; so I started to cry, *loudly*.

Finally, the neighbors spotted me. "Where's *Rescue 911* when you need them?" I thought. The neighbors seemed puzzled by my dilemma. One of the brightest of the bunch contacted my Uncle K., who rescued me. Then I got to go stay at my Grammy's. That was fun.

I'm still paying penance for that episode. Now my humans put me in jail when they go on vacation. Doesn't seem fair.

Clancy

Dog's Name: **Clancy**
Breed: **Golden Retriever**
Age: **4 years**
Sex: **Female**
Owner: **Sandy Beall**
Location: **Michigan**
Damage: **$500**

I must admit, I have a bad habit that I cannot get rid of. I chew and/or swallow things whole. It all started early on with socks. Later, I moved to more exotic items. I really lucked out when my humans had some workers in to replace a door. They left a box of single-edged razor blades on the floor and I struck gold!

I got them into the family room, chewed them to bits and swallowed most of them. If only the workers hadn't called back to say they couldn't find the box, my owners never would have known.

They found a few pieces I left behind, and then I had to go through all sorts of things at the vet. I got an X ray and they saw all the pieces, from my throat to my butt.

They put me on a bread-and-milk diet and I got to eat huge meals several times a day, but all the razor-blade pieces just lodged in my stomach. So, they were going to do surgery to get them out and had me fast for a day, and guess what—I pooped them *all* out overnight!

I don't know why they were so ecstatic.

My most recent escapade was with a towel. My owners always used it to dry my feet off when I came inside, so I finally got it one day, after they left. I tore off a 10-by-10-inch piece of the corner.

Boy, am I a *big* dog, because I swallowed the piece whole! Well, it created a blockage, and all I could do was puke and heave and get dehydrated.

Back I went to the vet, and X rays again, and there was the towel in my stomach. This time they operated and removed it. I think it had an "H" on the corner of it—Holiday Inn maybe?

I'm finally all recovered from my surgery. I just can't figure out why my mom was so sad when she wrote the check for $500 to the vet.

CHAPTER 15
Beyond Categorization

Beastie, bottom; Goose, top

Dog's Name: **Beastie**
Breed: **Peek-a-Poo**
Age: **Puppy**
Sex: **Male**
Owner: **Jean Scholefield**
Location: **Deptford, New Jersey**
Damage: **$100**

My name is Beastie and I am now a mature and sophisticated 13-year-old Peek-a-Poo. In my youth, however, I was a bit on the wild side. Mother often said I lived up to my name.

Grandmom's living room was neatly decorated and (according to Mommy) most of the area had been "puppy-proofed." Whatever that means. Grandpop is an avid hunter. So, he had lots of stuffed dead things around the house. One particular goose caught my eye—a trophy Canadian Snow Goose mounted on a piece of driftwood. Grandmom thought it looked pretty and had placed it in front of the fireplace. It was just standing there looking at me. I really thought it was being rude for not talking to me when I barked at it. What nerve to just stand there and stare into space, as if I didn't even exist!

What that goose needed was a good lesson about proper respect for dogs. So, I gave him a little nip on the leg. Can you believe that nasty old goose didn't even flinch? Well, I sure couldn't! No goose was going make a fool out of me!

I started biting both his feet. Biting and chewing and pulling until I bit into something very strange. After carefully surveying Mr. Goose (post-attack), I discovered that his legs and feet were nothing but wire. This goose wasn't real at all! Cautiously, I approached the pieces of leg that I had dismembered. They really didn't smell like a goose. In fact, they smelled a little bit like my rawhide treats. Being a canine with a healthy appetite, I couldn't help but wonder if they would also taste like my rawhides. So, I ate and ate and ate. Do you know, the taste wasn't really like rawhide—it tasted more like chicken!

The next morning, Grandmom and Mommy woke up and, boy, were they upset. They were frantic, in fact. They were moaning and cursing and picking up the goose and moving it around the room.

Grandmom just kept saying to Mommy, "If your father sees this, he'll never let that dog back in this house." I really couldn't imagine what *dog* they were talking about. They were holding a goose, not a dog!

Then Grandmom suddenly got very happy. She ran to her craft box and pulled out some green, mossy looking stuff. She starting putting it on the piece of driftwood where Mr. Goose was standing. Grandmom wrapped that mossy stuff all over the wire where the goose's legs used to be. Then she put it right back next to the fireplace, exactly where it had been in the first place.

They never mentioned to Grandpop what they had done to the goose and he never even noticed. In fact, it wasn't until I was *six years old* that Grandpop actually noticed that old goose.

Boy, was he mad!!! Funny thing, though, Mommy and Grandmom were just laughing and laughing the entire time Grandpop was yelling!

They just kept saying through their laughter, "It's been like that for more than *five years!*"

Oh well, humans . . . you gotta love 'em!

Cleo

Dog's Name: **Cleo**
Breed: **English Springer Spaniel**
Age: **1 year**
Sex: **Female**
Owners: **Victoria Tong and Chuck Bennett**
Location: **Ohio**
Damage: **A Glowing Snout**

My mom and dad scuba dive, but, being in Ohio, they dive in old rock quarries a lot. Several of the quarries have places to camp, so me and my brother Tsar got to sleep in a tent a lot during those early days!

Camping is great; you can run around mooching hot dogs and other goodies from the other campers. You just have to look friendly and kind of sad. We had that part down pat.

But I stray. Mom and Dad like to dive at night. I can't imagine what there is to see in a stupid old quarry at night, but, hey, to each his own. Diving at night requires the use of a lot of flashlights and these really cool little sticks. When you bend the stick it starts to glow green, just like lightning bugs!

Well, I just had to investigate one of the lightning bug sticks. I found one and snuck around to the back of the tent. Quietly, I opened the package up. Then, dumb old Tsar tried to take it away. I held on to it like grim death and growled. I snarled and bared my teeth. He wasn't about to get *my* treasure. He tried again; I growled some more and then I bit down a bit too hard! The guts started to leak out in my mouth! Yuck!

I spit, I shook, I spread all of the guts all over my jowls and face. I ran to find Mom . . . She was just getting out of the water and started laughing at me. She called me the "Devil Dog of the Deep!"

I was humiliated; I was going to glow all night. Tsar tried to cheer me up. He said I looked cool and that maybe we should go on the mooching tour.

You know, the old stupid butt was right. Everyone thought I looked really cool and the number of goodies was impressive.

Mom said I couldn't have anymore lightning bug sticks and she made me sleep outside that night. She said I was too bright a night-light.

Guiness

Dog's Name: **Guiness**
Breed: **American Staffordshire Terrier**
Age: **1 year**
Sex: **Male**
Owner: **Bridgette Kersten-Riggs**
Location: **Oklahoma**
Damage: **$1,000**

Dad left and went on vacation, leaving Mom here to take care of me and the other members of my pack, Ashley and Mitzi. We didn't want her to feel lonely, so we decided to make a few changes.

First, before Dad left, I had to chew up his motorcycle boots to try to keep him from leaving. I left designer doggie teeth marks on each one, making it a unique piece of art. He must have liked it 'cause he made quite a fuss.

Then, after he was gone and Mom was all alone with us, we decided to cheer her up and keep her busy. It was the 4th of July and all these loud noises were scaring poor Ashley and Mitzi.

So I slid off the couch and landed on my back and licked Ashley's big beautiful ears. She said, "Hey I have an idea," and we went into the compost bin and stole all the corncobs from dinner. They were still soaked in butter—mmmmmm! They were great! Ashley sure knows how to scrounge up some tasty morsels.

Meanwhile, Mitzi licked the butter off of a cob. Then I noticed that one of Mom's guests left her shoes on the floor. A nice pair of leather sandals! I munched the left one. Then I was caught. Everyone left except this one friend of hers, Monica, and she brought over this little blonde mop named Ginger. They stayed the night.

Well, I got to sleep upstairs with Mom! She said this was to keep me from jumping on the guest, but I got her the next morning—right on the head and then on the bladder. It was so much fun watching her scream and squirm!

Later that day, Mom was cleaning. This was bad news because I hate the vacuum, the broom, and the mop! I bark at 'em, chase 'em, and bite 'em! Well, not the vacuum—I just bark at it. It's still kinda scary.

Mom doesn't understand that cleaning is bad. It takes away all the good smells and replaces them with some nasty, icky smell. Humans don't appreciate the wonders of smells like we do. Sad! They don't know what they are missing.

Well, later that day, Mom was doing laundry. I snuck past her and went upstairs. Hey! It wasn't my fault—the gate was open!

First, I found a stuffed toy and shredded it. Hmm, that stuffing was so much fun, I decided go for something bigger . . . a pillow-back chair! I ripped the arms off and stuffing went everywhere!!! I got caught when the stuffing was falling over the stairs as Mom walked by downstairs. She screamed something about snow.

Anyway, I got in trouble and got stuck outside for a while all alone. I cried and screamed till she finally let me back in. After all, I was separated from my Ashley and Mitzi was laughing at me. She said that I need to learn manners or I'll be going to something called school.

Patch, left; Bear, right

Dog's Name: **Bear**
Breed: **Chow Chow**
Age: **2 years**
Sex: **Male**
Owner: **Lisa Ann Beattie**
Location: **Santa Barbara, California**
Damage: **Terrified Possum**

My brother Patch and I were born on the same day a year apart. He's a Welsh Springer Spaniel and Chocolate Lab mix.

But this story is about me and my Uncle Spock, who is a five-year-old Schipperke. This happened after we all moved in with Grandma and Uncle Spock. But I've been very busy trying to learn how to sit at the door and not bark when we have visitors, so I haven't had time to write!

One beautiful Santa Barbara evening, my uncle and I were enjoying the out-of-doors (in our backyard), when my mommy heard me barking very strangely.

Now, Chows bark strangely anyway, but these were short not-unhappy yipping noises she had never heard before. So she sent Daddy out to investigate. That's his job.

Daddy came running back in and made her come out to see us. He didn't tell her what was going on. We had been playing possum tossin'! But it was all over with by the time Mommy arrived. She never gets to see us have fun with wild animals.

But it sure was great! Daddy saw me grab the possum and swing him high in the air. Then I'd let go! The possum would fly quite a few feet, and then it was Spock's turn. But he couldn't toss very far; he just kind of flipped him over! We did it over and over again, and yipped with joy!

Daddy thought the possum was dead, and that's when he went to get Mommy, but the possum was just playin' possum!

How Sticky Can Glue Be?

Dog's Name: **Liesl**
Breed: **Dachshund**
Age: **1 year**
Sex: **Female**
Owner: **Jeanne Burnham**
Location: **Spain**
Damage: **Doggy Dignity Destroyed**

I was not a pretty sight at the time of this event—my mom called me "Mangy Mutt" because of the way I looked. One day, I went to the garage. As my mom was working, I was poking my nose around, as Dachshunds usually do, and ended up with a strip of glue attached to me.

Now, this wasn't just a piece of packing tape, but glue used to seal up holes in the roof. My mom didn't know what I was into, and when she tried to remove the strip she got glue on her. While I was prancing around trying to help her she grabbed me with her glued hand. Can you imagine what we looked like?

I had one end of the strip on my paw, the middle part on my ear, and the end part on my side. My back had Mom's hand stuck to it. After some struggle, she managed to get the strip off and me to the vet, but he couldn't help us too much.

We went home and I had to have a bath. *Ugh!* Anyway, that didn't get the glue off, either. She kicked me outside and told me to go play for awhile while she thought of the next step.

I thought I would surprise her and have the glue gone by the time she came out, but little did I know that I wasn't really helping at all! As I was rolling around, I collected leaves, grass and dirt all over me and they wouldn't come off because of the glue.

Needless to say, I was a mess and I can truly understand why no one would let me jump up on the couch. No one ever said Dachshunds were dumb—just lacking in common dog sense. My mom's friend thought I should be sent under all the beds to collect the dust bunnies. Now that's going a bit too far, don't you think?

The Ultimate Tail of Woe

Dog's Name: **Shelly**
Breed: **Mix**
Age: **Puppy**
Sex: **Female**
Owners: **Dennis and Judy Fiddler**
Location: **South Carolina**
Damage: **$10**

I have committed the ultimate bad dog crime. It's really not my fault. Mom says I'm a "klep-toe-maniac." I'm really an Australian Shepherd mix, but if being that "klep-toe" thing keeps me out of trouble, I'm keeping my mouth shut.

Anyway, I like to take things off of counters, chairs, laundry baskets, you know, things that belong to other people. I really like for people to chase me and try to get their stuff back, but if they don't see me, then I just chew their stuff up.

The other day, on Mom's desk, there was this yellow rectangular-looking thing wrapped in shiny plastic. Plastic is my second favorite thing to eat. I waited until everyone else was asleep and then I took the rectangular thing off the desk and ate it up.

It was hard plastic inside the yellow cover and I really had to work at it. I did notice that on the yellow cardboard stuff there was a picture of another dog.

The next morning, when Mom found all the leftover pieces from my feast, she just laughed and wondered if any other bad dogs had ever eaten *Tails of Woe*, The Bad Dog Video.

About the Bad Dog Chronicles Gang

Andrew

Andrew is the Webmaster for the Bad Dog Chronicle's Web site. He is a handsome 12-year-old Pekingnese who has a cute cyber girlfriend named Mitzi. His hobbies are escaping weekly from the backyard in search of doggie babes, cleaning Emily's eyeballs and spending time with his pet hermit crab, Shelly.

Emily is the primary "Bad Dog Story Critic." She is a voluptuous

Emily

7-year-old Lhasa Apso and is currently single and available. Her hobbies include scarfing down anything that is beef, bossing around Maggie and Andrew and being the cutest and sassiest Lhasa around.

Maggie is the dog who started it all. She destroyed a brand-new hide-a-bed love seat given to the family by Grandma and removed a 2-square-foot area of linoleum from the middle of the kitchen floor. She is a plump 4-year-old Golden Retriever and is one of the sweetest dogs around. Her hobbies include catching frogs, giving wet kisses and eating. Maggie's version of the events that kicked off the Bad Dog Chronicles follows:

Dog's Name: **Maggie**

Breed: **Golden Retriever**

Age: **2 years**

Sex: **Female**

Owner: **The Brown Family**

Location: **Tallahassee, Florida**

Damage: **$500**

Oh, Grandma gave "me" this lovely new love seat! The only problem was it needed a little breaking in! The stuffing just wasn't settled in the right spots yet. Andrew and Emily said that I shouldn't even be sitting on the love seat. What did they know? Boy, had they forgotten their puppyhood days or what?

Mitzi

Maggie

The Brown Family

Why would Mom and Dad put this love seat in "our" room if it wasn't for "us" to use?

I pounced on the love seat. It was springy! I rolled on my back on it so it would be more broken in. A good comfy love seat needs a few hairs and doggie smells on it.

Hmmmm. It still needs a little adjusting here and . . . there . . . Tug on it here . . . Scratch it a little here . . . and . . . What's this white stuff? Where did it come from?

I know what I did next was wrong, but I was only a puppy with lots of puppy hyperness!

I pulled chunks and chunks of the white stuff out of the love seat. I scattered it all over the room and bit off chunks of the cushions. I was caught up in my puppy frenzy!

I asked Emily and Andrew if they thought Mom and Dad would notice that I had sat on the couch. They just shook their heads. I curled up on "my" comfy couch and took a nice long puppy nap!

Two days later, early in the morning, I got the sudden urge to dig! It would have been okay if I was outside, but I wasn't. The urge was uncontrollable!! It was that puppy hyperness again!

I started digging and digging and digging. It was hard work and I wasn't getting anywhere!! Finally, I made a small hole in the flooring. It's just a dog's natural response to make a small hole bigger.

The linoleum was chewy and kind of tasty! I had made a hole with a diameter of about 2 feet when my dad came into the room. The pulling of linoleum was making a popping sound that gave me away. Boy was he mad at me! Do you think it was because the hole was in the very middle of the kitchen floor or because the linoleum was in the brand-new kitchen of our new home??

Well, the story is not over quite yet . . . read on . . .

Mom and Dad worked for hours patching my hole. Dad grumbled something about it costing too much money to replace the entire flooring.

It was very hard to patch the hole I made but they did a good job. I had to really search to find it again. But I did find it and made a hole again! Needless to say, they were not very understanding this second time!

So those are some of the major reasons why I got sent to boarding school that summer. Bummer!

Emily and Andrew's Comment: When Maggie started tearing up the couch and digging at the linoleum, we told her she should not be doing that but she did not listen. We never did things like that when we were pups. We were sorry to see her go to boarding school, but we have to admit she did return with a few more IQ points.

Please Share with Us

If you have a Bad Dog story that you would like to share with us, please submit it to us on the Internet at www.baddogs.com. We would like to publish another volume of great Bad Dog tales in the future and would love to consider using your story.

We'd also love to hear any feedback about this book. You can e-mail us at bowwow@baddogs.com.

Thanks again to the hundreds of dogs from all around the world who submitted stories and pictures for this book. A big BOWWOW to you all!

Baddest Dog in the Book

Vote for who you think is the baddest dog in the book at bowwow@ baddogs.com! Voters' names will go into a drawing for the Howell book of the winner's choice. Five winners will be drawn. Only one vote per family (that includes dogs!).

The baddest dog in the book will receive an engraved plaque proclaiming him or her the Baddest Dog in the World. Winners will be notified during National Dog Month, 2000.

Printed in the USA
CPSIA information can be obtained
at www.ICGtesting.com
JSHW012016140824
68134JS00025B/2448

9 781620 457641